The Quest
for the Rusyn Soul

The Quest
for the Rusyn Soul

The Politics of Religion and Culture in Eastern Europe and in America, 1890–World War I

Keith P. Dyrud

Philadelphia
The Balch Institute Press
London and Toronto: Associated University Presses

Associated University Presses
440 Forsgate Drive
Cranbury, NJ 08512

Associated University Presses
25 Sicilian Avenue
London WC1A 2QH, England

Associated University Presses
P.O. Box 39, Clarkson Pstl. Stn.
Mississauga, Ontario,
L5J 3X9 Canada

The paper used in this publication meets the requirements
of the American National Standard for Permanence of Paper
for Printed Library Materials Z39.48-1984.

Library of Congress Cataloging-in-Publication Data

Dyrud, Keith P.
  The quest for the Rusyn soul : the politics of religion and
culture in Eastern Europe and in America, 1890–World War I / Keith
P. Dyrud.
     p.   cm.
  Includes bibliographical references and index.
  ISBN 0-944190-10-3 (alk. paper)
  1. Ruthenians—Ethnic identity.   2. Ruthenians—Religion.
3. Europe, Eastern—Politics and government.   4. United States—
Church history—20th century.   I. Title.
DJK28.R87D97   1992
305.891'791—dc20   91-77488
                                                                         CIP

PRINTED IN THE UNITED STATES OF AMERICA

To Grace,
my wife and colleague

Contents

Preface

Various views of Rusyn history illustrate a conflict among competing philosophies of history. Some historians suggest that history leads to an ultimate end or goal; some advocate a correct path to follow to achieve that end. With that philosophy of history it is possible for historical figures to have made mistakes. Mistakes are policies or behavior which detour a people from that goal.

Ukrainian historians are inclined to view the history of the Rusyns from that perspective. The "goal" of history from their perspective is a developed Ukrainian identity and homeland for all Ukrainians. For these historians, Rusyns are Ukrainians. Thus Rusyn leaders who were Russophiles, Pro-Polish, or Magyarones made mistakes and distracted the Rusyns from the correct but undiscovered path. Rusyns who were searching for a "Rusyn" identity were also in error but their error was not so far from the correct path.

Some historians find patterns in the past so they feel they can anticipate events, or fill in gaps in historical knowledge and occasionally judge the appropriateness of some past behavior. Some historians argue that human events are determined by scientific principles and those principles are discoverable by historians.

I am not going to take sides in the "grand scheme of history" argument. I do not deny any of the above possibilities but I do not feel I am in a position to make awesome judgments about history. I cannot discover any "end" to history until that "end" occurs and is called "the present." Thus neither Rusyn history nor any other people's past should be judged by faithfulness to an objective which was discovered or determined after the fact. Instead, humans can be seen as "wanderers through time" with historians chronicling those wanderings and making judgments about them.

The Quest
for the Rusyn Soul

Introduction: The Rusyns

The Rusyns live in Europe on the border between East and West. This geographical fact has shaped their history and continues to influence their existence. The Rusyns are East Slavs. Russian historians often identify them as "Russians," and Ukrainians often identify them as "Ukrainians." Some historians identify the Rusyns as a unique people.[1]

A border also divided the Rusyns. Before the division of Poland in 1772, the Galician Rusyns lived in Poland and the Subcarpathian Rusyns lived in northeastern Hungary. The Rusyns in Subcarpathia were separated geographically from their kin in Galicia by the Carpathian mountain range. They were also separated by cultural influences. The Rusyns south of the Carpathians are influenced by Hungarian and Slovak culture. North of the Carpathians the Rusyns were influenced by Polish and Ukrainian culture.

The "border" nature of the Rusyns' culture is most noticeable in their church. Their church has become the symbol of their existence. They were "Greek Catholics." The "Greek" does not stand for "Greek" as a nationality, it stands for "Greek Orthodox Christianity" or, more appropriately, "Eastern Orthodox Christianity." The "Catholic" in the term does stand for "Catholic," specifically the "Catholic" church with its headquarters in Rome.

In the sixteenth and seventeenth centuries these Rusyns were converted from Orthodoxy to Catholicism. But most Rusyns were illiterate peasants, and they were attached to the traditional practices of their faith. They did not wish to adopt the Latin rite. Compromises were worked out at the Union of Brest in 1595 and the Union of Uzhhorod in 1646. These compromises allowed the Rusyns to continue their traditional religious practices, but their bishops owed their allegiance to the Catholic pope.[2]

This "practical" accommodation in religious practices merely reflected a shift in the political border in Eastern Europe. Prior to the sixteenth century these Rusyns had been oriented toward the East. Since the seventeenth century, the Rusyns in Hungary and Poland lived in the "Latin" West. In 1772, Austria annexed

Galicia. Since then, the Rusyns, both Galicians and Subcarpathians, lived in the Austro-Hungarian empire.[3]

The disposition of these Rusyn areas then became "the Rusyn question." In examining the cultural options of the Rusyns in Eastern Europe and in the United States, this study will focus on the Russian interests in the Rusyn Question. In so doing it is important not to overlook the Hungarian and Ukrainian perspectives in this "quest for the Rusyn soul." All parties involved seemed to be anticipating the Wilsonian principle of self-determination. They operated as if the cultural orientation of the Rusyn population would some day determine whether the Rusyn areas would be annexed to Russia or be directed toward some other cultural objective.

Present day scholars generally study the Rusyns in Galicia and the Rusyns in Subcarpathia separately. It is true that both groups, while living in the same empire, did not share a common existence. But there have been several times in the last 200 years when the Rusyns themselves thought they had a common heritage and made some effort to work together to establish a single Rusyn culture. One of those instances occurred after the death of Andrei Bachyns'kyi, the Greek Catholic Bishop of Prešov (in Subcarpathia). The Greek Catholic Metropolitanate of Galicia was reestablished in Peremysl about the time Bachyns'kyi died in 1809. Bachyns'kyi and others had recognized the common heritage of the Greek Catholic Rusyns and had worked tirelessly to join Galician and Subcarpathian Rusyns into a single metropolia. It would have been reasonable to place the Subcarpathian diocese under the metropolia of Peremysl. However, Hungarian exclusivity prevented such ecclesiastical foundation for ethnic unity.[4]

The above incident occurred before the period covered by this study. Within the scope of this study there were two occasions when the Rusyns from both sides of the Carpathians investigated the possibility of establishing a working relationship. Chapter 1 briefly surveys cross-Carpathian Rusyn communication in the period after 1848 when national identity became such a powerful force. The second occasion occurred among the Rusyn immigrants to North America. Rusyns from both sides of the Carpathians emigrated to the United States and many of them settled in the same communities. In those communities early missionaries such as Father John Voliansky from Galicia and Father Alexis Toth from Subcarpathia established parishes that had members from both sides of the Carpathians.[5]

This study does not focus on the common interests of the two Rusyn groups; in fact, it focuses on their differences. In spite of early attempts at cooperation, the differences prevailed. Many of the problems faced by these Rusyns were problems that were shared by both groups of Rusyns, but the resolutions of these problems differed. When research focuses exclusively on the Galicians or exclusively on the Subcarpathians, the researcher often underemphasizes the commonality of the problems and generally is critical of the "other" Rusyns for not joining to solve the problem "their way."

Some Rusyns, especially those from Subcarpathia, suspected they were Rusyns with no grander identity, but many others suggested the Rusyns harbored a "greater" heritage. There were many players seeking the "Rusyn soul." They included Russian Pan-Slavists who advocated a Russian identity, and the Russian Orthodox church, which reminded the Rusyns of their sixteenth-century Orthodox heritage. They included the Ukrainians who suggested that Rusyns were Ukrainians. The Ukrainians were not so concerned if the Rusyns were Greek Catholic or Orthodox. (The Ukrainian Orthodox church was founded after the period under discussion.) The Ukrainian identification was more readily acceptable in Galicia than Subcarparthia.[6]

The Hungarians were also determined to win the soul of the Subcarpathian Rusyns. The Hungarians had no interest in the Galicians; in fact, they had little interest in Rusyns as Rusyns. They insisted that all citizens of Hungary be Magyars (Hungarians) and therefore the Rusyns should speak Magyar.[7] Even when the Subcarpathian Rusyns migrated to the United States, the Hungarian government wished them to be identified as Magyars. Within Hungary the Rusyns shared territory with fellow Slavs identified as Slovaks. The Slovaks identified the Rusyns as "Greek Catholic Slovaks" but made little attempt to change them. Especially in the United States, the Slovaks often acted as helpful brothers to the Rusyns.[8]

The Catholic church had an interest in the Rusyns from both sides of the Carpathians. The Roman hierarchy was determined that no Catholics—Greek or Latin—should be lost to the church. In the new world such an exodus seemed likely if the Rusyns were not allowed to practice their traditions. There the American Catholic church was determined that only the Latin rite should be transplanted to the United States.[9]

These contestants in the quest for the Rusyns' soul were activists whose programs created an environment of international intrigue. The significance of these events was heightened because Europe was dividing into armed camps. These contestants for the Rusyn soul were also divided between those two alliances led by Russia on one side and the Habsburg Empire on the other. All these events took place in the long shadow being cast by events leading to the First World War. Thus the Rusyn soul was sought by two empires that wished to control the border occupied by those Rusyns.[10]

The quest for the allegiance of the Rusyns was a reasonable one. The ethnic or national identity of these people was in doubt even by the Rusyns themselves. They could have been a separate nationality or they could have been Polish, Hungarian, Russian, or Ukrainian.

For several decades prior to the outbreak of the First World War, Russian Slavonic Benevolent Societies, the Holy Synod of the Russian Orthodox church, and the Russian government attempted to demonstrate that these Rusyns were ethnic Russians. These Russian institutions also sought to convert the Rusyns to Orthodoxy and convince them they were members of the Great Russian family.[11]

This Russian cultural mission concentrated its activities in Galicia, but extended them to Subcarpathia and to the Rusyn immigrants in the United States. Russian activities among citizens of the Austro-Hungarian Empire naturally caused concern among the leadership in that empire. It also became apparent that Russia wished to annex the Rusyn territories, while Austria and Hungary wished to hold on to them.

Officially and privately, the Russians tried to win the sympathy and support of the East European Slavs (not just the Rusyns) for the Russian cause in the competition with the Habsburg Empire prior to the First World War. In some cases, especially among the Rusyns in eastern Galicia and the Carpathian Mountain region, the Russians went so far as to try to convince the Slavic population that it was Russian with a Russian cultural heritage, and that these Slavs should strive for "reunification" with their motherland.[12]

Between 1880 and the outbreak of the First World War, a large number of these Rusyns immigrated to the United States. The American immigration authorities, however, often did not recognize them as a nationality so these Rusyns were often identified as Poles (since many were from Galicia, which had a large Polish population when it was under Austria), or Hungarians (since many were from Subcarpathia, which was under Hungary), or

Austrians (because the entire area from which they came was within the Austrian Empire), or Russians (because the language they spoke was often identified as Russian). Very few were ever identified as Ukrainian, but most of the area from which they came is now a part of Ukraine and the people are now generally identified as Ukrainian. Probably three hundred thousand to four hundred thousand Rusyns immigrated to the United States before 1914.[13]

By 1890, both Russia and Austria recognized the strategic importance of the Rusyns to the future interests of their respective empires. The Austrian government was interested in the solution to the Rusyn question because a pro-Russian solution would gravely threaten the integrity of Austrian Imperial territory. As a result, the Austrian government supported the Ukrainian movement as the most effective way to reverse the Russification trend among the Rusyns.

Russia responded by initiating an intensive cultural drive in both Europe and America to encourage Rusyns to become Russians. Their chief instrument for this cultural drive was the Russian Orthodox church.

The Austro-Hungarian Empire tried to counter the Russian effort in a number of ways. In Galicia the Austrian government made sporadic efforts to improve the lot of the Rusyns in relation to the Poles who controlled the government in Galicia. The Austrians also lent encouragement to the developing Ukrainian movement in Galicia. The Ukrainian movement was in competition with the Russian cultural effort and was thus a useful tool in Austria's opposition to "Russian cultural imperialism."[14]

In Subcarpathia, however, the Hungarians determined the strategy, and their approach was to Magyarize the Rusyn population by eliminating Rusyn institutions such as schools. Their method also called for Magyar control of the hierarchy of the Greek Catholic church, which represented the Rusyn people. When this approach was extended to the immigrants in America, it was not as easily executed. Magyar efforts, directed by the Hungarian prime minister in Budapest, resulted in intrigues designed to frustrate the growing Rusyn national identification among the immigrants in America.[15]

The Greek Catholic church maintained a central position in the lives of the Rusyn people. The Greek Catholic church is essentially a church of the Rusyn people. Its authority is based on Unia agreements between the formerly Orthodox church leaders of the Rusyn people and the Roman Catholic church. The first agreement, which placed the Galician Rusyns in communion with Rome, was signed at Brest in 1596. The Rusyns in northern Hungary came under Roman Catholic authority by an oral agreement at Uzhhorod in 1646 that was later confirmed by written agreements in 1664 and 1713. These agreements allowed the Rusyns to maintain their Eastern church traditions, which included worship services with Church Slavonic as the liturgical language. The parish priests could continue to be married, and the priests could continue to administer the sacrament of confirmation at baptism. These were traditions that obviously differed from those of the Roman church where the liturgical language was Latin, the priests were celibate, and the bishop, not the priest, administered the sacrament of confirmation.[16]

Throughout the centuries that followed, the Greek Catholic church remained uniquely the church of the Rusyn people. This church received some legal protection and some ecclesiastical protection. As a result the church became the bulwark against assimilation of the Rusyns by the Roman Catholic majorities in both Galicia and Hungary. These legal and ecclesiastical rights were greatly strengthened under Maria Theresa and Joseph II who, in theory, made the Greek Catholic church coequal to the Roman Catholic church.[17]

As long as the Austrian government had control over the Rusyn provinces, the Rusyns had some chance of maintaining their identity as a separate nationality. However, in the years following the revolutions of 1848, Galicia received a Polish governor and in 1867 Hungary received the power to govern itself. From then on governmental policies, especially in Hungary, were often directed at absorbing the Rusyn peoples into the majority population.[18]

Interest in the cultural and political destiny of the Rusyns in Galicia and Subcarpathia motivated the quest for the Rusyn soul. Between 1848, and the First World War, 1914, this interest expressed itself in a variety of proposals. The Polish population in Galicia wished to absorb the Rusyn population. The Hungarians in Hungary also wished to Magyarize the Rusyn population in northern Hungary. The Russian government, the Russian Orthodox church, and numerous Slavic societies planned to absorb the Rusyns into the mainstream of Great Russian culture in preparation for future annexation. The Rusyns themselves, especially for a while after 1848, wished to form a unified Rusyn state with autonomy directly under the Austrian monarch. This

Rusyn movement, however, remained divided by the Carpathian mountains, which divided Austrian Galicia from Hungarian Subcarpathia. In Galicia the Rusyns gradually split into a pro-Russian movement and a pro-Ukrainian movement with the pro-Ukrainian movement becoming a popular majority movement. The Ukrainians wished to unite the Rusyn people with the people of eastern Ukraine, which was under Russian control at that time.[19]

While the first attempts to unite the Rusyns with Russian culture and Orthodoxy occurred in Galicia, the most successful endeavor occurred in the United States. The first conversion in the new world took place in Minneapolis at the St. Mary's Greek Catholic Church under the direction of the Subcarpathian priest, Father Alexis G. Toth.[20] The conversion of St. Mary's Greek Orthodox Catholic Church to Russian Orthodoxy began a movement that led to the conversion of over one-third of the Rusyn immigrants.

In view of this cultural conflict centering on the Rusyns, it may be well to inquire: "Who were the Rusyns?" They were not Poles, Hungarians, or Russians. They would have had to change in some way to become one of those three options: 1) to become Poles (in Galicia), they would have had to adopt the Polish language and become Roman Catholic. 2) To become Magyars (in Subcarpathia), they would have had to adopt the Magyar language. 3) To become Russians (in either Galicia or Subcarpathia), it was not quite so clear. They should become Orthodox, but not necessarily. They should adopt Muscovite Russian as their literary language since their spoken language was a "vulgar dialect" of Great Russian.

To become Ukrainian, however, required no change at all. They could be Greek Catholic, Roman Catholic, or Orthodox. Their language was acceptable as it was spoken: dialectical differences were no problem and the written literary language was only a standardized version of the spoken language. Indeed Ukrainians have consistently identified Rusyns as Ukrainians. However, during the period under discussion, some Galicians and most Subcarpathian Rusyns did not wish to be so identified. (The Rusyns in the Prešov area of Subcarpathia could also have been Slovaks if they had so chosen.) So who were the Rusyns? They were Greek Catholic Slavs of peasant stock who lived in Galicia (and Bukovina) and Subcarpathia. That definition, while adequate for this study, is not comprehensive because there were communities of Rusyns elsewhere in Eastern Europe, and there were also some Slovaks, Magyars, Romanians, and Croatians who were Greek Catholics.

The Rusyn community in the United States took seriously President Wilson's concept of "self-determination" and consulted with the president, hoping to aid him in making a decision on the new boundaries in Eastern Europe at the close of the war. The policy of self-determination reinforced the judgment that it did make a difference who the Rusyns thought they were, not only in Eastern Europe but also in America. So it seems that Russian cultural policy had been founded on astute reasoning. However, by 1918, the Bolshevik Revolution had taken Russia out of the war, alienated her from the victorious Allies, and eliminated all chance that Russian interests would be favorably considered at the Paris Peace Conference. Perhaps the fact that the Bolshevik Revolution nullified a carefully executed plan of Russian cultural imperialism has led historians to overlook a very interesting and unique aspect of Russian foreign policy.

1

The Development of National Awareness among the Rusyns in the Austrian Empire

The Rusyns in eastern Galicia and Subcarpathia in the nineteenth century were peasants. These peasants had few ideas concerning the nature of their language or the identity of their nationality. If there were "intellectuals" among them, they were generally priests or, in a few cases, civil servants. In many cases these civil servants were also children of clergy so there was a clerical dimension to the world view of the secular intellectuals as well.[1] The language of discourse among the peasants was an unrecognized slavic language. Some Polish scholars wished to include eastern Galicia with Polish western Galicia so they categorized the language as a variation of the Polish peasant speech.[2] The language of discourse among the intellectuals and ruling elites was not the peasant language, at least not in the first half of the nineteenth century. The intellectuals would speak German or Polish in Galicia and Magyar or German in Subcarpathia. Latin and, occasionally, Church Slavonic were also options, especially for the priests.

At that time some Galician Rusyn intellectuals accepted the Polish position on language and nationality. The Rusyn priests were less inclined to accept the Polish "option" of nationality because the Rusyns were Greek Catholic and the Poles were invariably Roman Catholic. Thus the Polish option was a threat to the Rusyns' rite. But the Rusyn civil servants were more inclined to identify with the Poles, even to the extent that they would attend a Roman Catholic church.[3] The Rusyn leaders in Galicia began to separate themselves from the Poles after the 1830 Polish revolt against Russian control in the Polish area occupied by Russia just to the north of Galicia. The Poles in Galicia sympathized with that revolt but the Rusyns were less interested.[4]

About 1832, three Rusyn intellectuals, Markiian Shashkevych,

Iakiv Holovats'kyi, and Ivan Vahylevych organized a group to search for a Rusyn identity. These three became known as the "Rusyn Triad." They discussed both the language question and the problem of national identity.[5] Markiian Shashkevych died in 1843 before his ideas on either issue were set so he became a hero to all sides in the future controversies. Ivan Vahylevych (who died in 1866) in later life felt that Rusyn cooperation with the Poles would best assure a future for the Galician Rusyns. Iakiv Holovats'kyi became a Russophile and eventually emigrated to Russia.[6]

Language and nationality were not easily identifiable in this formative period of Rusyn culture. It is beyond the scope of this work to evaluate the development of the language and nationality question except in some cases where it intersects with the broader issue of Great Power interest in the Rusyns.

In 1835 and again in 1839, Mikhail Pogodin, a Russian Pan-Slav, suggested a program that would incorporate the Rusyns into the Russian Empire. Actually he did not limit his interests to the Rusyns. He suggested that "all the Slavs to the Adriatic Sea sympathize with her [Russia]."[7] Thus he argued that Russia should adopt an activistic foreign policy dedicated to the division of Austria and the incorporation of the Austrian Empire's slavic population.

No official Russian policy was based on Pogodin's ideas at that time, but his ideas became the central theme of the later Pan-Slavic movement. This movement, however, did achieve some status with Imperial Russian policy makers by the turn of the century. While Pogodin's objectives were clearly political, he did not have an immediate political impact on the Rusyns in either Galicia or Subcarpathia. Pogodin was probably influential in suggesting that the Russian language could become the literary language for the Rusyns and that linguistic suggestion was acceptable to some Rusyn intellectuals. While Pogodin's ideas did appeal to some Rusyn leaders, these same leaders also recognized that cooperation with the Austrian Empire was in their national interest for the foreseeable future.[8]

Pogodin's Pan-Slavic ideas were shared with some Slovak intellectuals who also influenced the Rusyn intellectuals. In 1842 a Slovak, Pavel Šafárik, published an ethnographic census of the Slavs that was used by Iakiv Holovats'kyi when he suggested that "of the total of 13,144,000 Ukrainians [Rusyns], 10,370,000 lived in Russia and 2,774,000 in Austria, of which 625,000 were in Hungary."[9] Holovats'kyi was recognizing the common relationship between the Rusyns on both sides of the Austrian-Russian border.

While Pogodin suggested that Russia should establish a foreign policy appealing to the Slavs outside its border, Jernei Kopitar, a Slovenian, offered a counter proposal to Austrian officials. Kopitar suggested that Austria should encourage the Rusyns in Galicia to identify with the Rusyns (Ukrainians) in Russia and encourage the Russian Ukrainians to distinguish themselves from the Russians. The next step would be for the Austrian government to encourage the Ukrainians to join with the Galicians to form a common homeland.[10] This idea developed into the Ukrainian idea later in the century but before 1848 it was just one of many possibilities.

The revolutionary year of 1848 was a watershed year in Europe. Throughout the continent revolutions sprang up as if they were spontaneous. These revolutions were generally liberal and nationalistic. Liberalism and nationalism had developed during the period of "enlightenment" and matured in the French Revolution. Even the conservative multinational Austrian Empire in East Central Europe was not immune to these upheavals.

The Austrians rejected the conservatism of the Metternich era and established a liberal parliament in Vienna. The Hungarians rejected the multinational dimension of the empire, wishing to establish a nationalistic Magyar-dominated nation under the guise of a liberal democracy. Such a democracy would have left little opportunity for Rusyn national development.

The Poles in Galicia had unsuccessfully revolted two years earlier so they were not in a position to engage in a full-scale revolution. They did, however, take full advantage of the revolutionary environment. They established Polish representation in Galicia and selected representatives to the Imperial parliament in Vienna.

It was this Polish activity that spread the spark of nationalism among a larger group of Rusyns in Galicia. By May 1848, the Rusyns established a Supreme Rusyn Council. This council was organized by Bishop Hryhorii Iakymovych, the Greek Catholic bishop of Lviv.[11] Another of the organizers of this council was a priest named Kuzems'kyi who was a member of the Stavropigian Institute in Lviv.[12]

This council was established by the Rusyns primarily to protect Rusyn interests in response to the Polish revolutionary movement. The Polish movement was demanding that Galicia be made a Polish state with Polish self-government. The Poles had set up their own council in Lviv on 15 April of that year, and this move spurred the Rusyns into action in a way that the Polish demonstrations had not.[13]

The council drafted a request to the emperor that included a number of articles requesting the increase of cultural autonomy for the Rusyns. The request significantly pointed out that the Rusyns were not Poles and should be treated separately from and equally with the Poles. Since over half of the peasant population in eastern Galicia was Rusyn, the Poles should not have the power to govern them.[14] It must have been of some embarrassment to the Rusyns that until 15 May all discussions and communications had been carried on in Polish. So on 15 May they began to correct the situation with the publication of the first Rusyn political newspaper, Zoria halytska.[15]

The council supported the unity of the Rusyn people in the Austrian Empire. Politically, however, the Rusyn Council was a very mild institution. It wished to develop some safeguards for Rusyn cultural autonomy against Polish dominance, but it did not represent political or economic revolutionaries. It strongly supported the Austrian central government since its resolutions asked the Austrian government to protect the Rusyns from Polish domination.

The situation in Subcarpathia was quite different. There the Rusyns observed the Hungarian uprising and the Slovak demonstrations and the founding of Slovak councils, but there was little organized political activity on the part of the Rusyns. Several individuals, such as Aleksander Dukhnovych and Adol'f Dobrians'kyi, did propose that the Rusyn lands on both sides of the Carpathian Mountains be united into a single Rusyn crown land. This idea was endorsed by the Supreme Rusyn Council in Lviv and was presented to Emperor Franz Joseph in Vienna, but other political factors prevented it from being implemented.[16]

The Russian occupation of Hungary in 1849, however, had a most significant impact on the national awakening of the Rusyns in Subcarpathia as well as Galicia. The Austrian government was not able to put down the Hungarian uprising in 1848, so Nicholas I of Russia agreed to send troops into Hungary to put down the revolution. Nicholas sent Field Marshall Prince Paskevich with almost 200,000 troops into Hungary in 1849.[17] These troops inevitably came into contact with the native Rusyns as they crossed through eastern Galicia and also with the Rusyns in Hungary.

This contact radically altered some Rusyns' view of the Russian people. Ioann Grigorevich Naumovich, a Galician Rusyn priest, was stationed in eastern Galicia as a tutor when the Russian troops passed through. He was later converted to Orthodoxy and became one of the prime architects of the "back to Orthodoxy" movement in Galicia. Naumovich made the observation that, contrary to popular opinion among the Rusyns and the Poles, the Russians were not savages capable only of drinking and robbing. On the contrary he discovered that they were good and warm-hearted.[18] Some Subcarpathian Rusyns made the same observations and noted that the Russians and Rusyns were of the same family, blood, and spirit.[19]

This interaction between the Russian soldiers and the Rusyn intellectuals created an alternative cultural and literary identity for some Rusyn intellectuals. This alternative identity provided a perspective from which Rusyn intellectuals could examine their own cultural identity. Some critically examined the Polonization of their heritage. The extent to which Polonization had occurred among the Rusyns in Galicia is exemplified by the early life of Mykhailo Kachkovs'kyi, who later became an important figure in the development of the Russophile movement.[20]

He was born in 1802, the son of a Greek Catholic priest and, of course, trained to be a priest himself. But he was diverted into the study of law and became a civil servant. During his student years he spoke Polish and spent his summers in the home of a Polish nobleman.[21] The only thing that kept him from being identified as Polish was his Greek Catholicism, and as will be noted later, it was his Greek Catholicism that limited his complete identification with Orthodox Russia.

After 1848, interest in non-Polish cultural activities rapidly increased and when the Supreme Rusyn Council was dissolved in 1851, a group of intellectuals organized the Galitsko-Ruska Matytsia. This *matica* (or learning society) was pro-Russian.[22] It is, perhaps, best to qualify that statement by suggesting that they were "linguistically" and, in some cases, culturally pro-Russian. These "Old Ruthenians" were also politically loyal to the Austrian Empire. They were politically conservative and could be called a "pro-government party."[23] This group also controlled the National Home in Lviv,[24] which served as a meeting place for interested Rusyns. It subscribed to a number of Russian and Galician journals and newspapers and had an extensive library available to the public. These members of the *matica* were known as the "St. George Clique," after the Greek Catholic cathedral in Lviv.[25]

For two decades following the 1848 awakening, the Russophile movement provided cultural direction for many Rusyn intellectuals in both Galicia and Subcarpathia. For the next two decades this pro-Russian movement increasingly became a Russian cultural movement and less an indigenous cultural movement with Russian sympathies. Perhaps the best way to observe this transformation among the Russophiles in Galicia is to review briefly the lives of the Russophiles' two most eminent leaders, Mykhailo Kachkovs'kyi and Ioann Grigorevich Naumovich. Kachkovs'kyi was the elder and the spiritual father to Naumovich. (The following biographical sketches will be presented adopting the tone of the original Russian Slavophile biographies.)

Mykhailo Kachkovs'kyi was born in 1802 in the village of Dubn, the son of the parish priest. He was, like most Rusyns in Galicia, a member of the Greek Catholic church.[26] He began his education to be a parish priest and demonstrated himself to be an outstanding student. But during his higher education in Lviv, he changed his occupation and studied law. After his schooling, he joined the civil service and was assigned to Sambor, south of Lviv. As a civil servant he took an active interest in the Rusyns in the Sambor area.[27]

Kachkovs'kyi had spent some of his youth in the home of a Polish lord. However, when he came to Sambor, he was confronted for the first time with the Polish suppression of the Rusyns. He began to identify himself with the Rusyn clerks, and he soon joined a Rusyn circle made up of Rusyn clerks and other local Rusyn intellectuals.

In 1833–34 Kachkovs'kyi took a trip to Switzerland and spent some time in Vienna. When he returned, he began to write songs and poetry. Kachkovs'kyi was then influenced by the developing movement among the Rusyn young people. This movement encouraged an examination of the Rusyns' cultural heritage. The Stavropigian Institute took advantage of this interest by publishing several brochures written by a young writer, Denis Zubritsko. Zubritsko linked the early Galician culture to the Russian (Kievan) princes and thereby linked Galician culture to Russian culture.[28]

These influences led Kachkovs'kyi to make a decisive break with the traditional practices of civil servants. He quit attending the Polish Catholic church and began to attend the Greek Catholic church. Such a step, no doubt, seriously limited his opportunities for promotion.[29]

The fateful year, 1848, was also a turning point in the life of

Kachkovs'kyi. All the crucial events of April and May of that year were unknown to Kachkovs'kyi because he was not in Lviv and he depended on the Polish press for news from Lviv. Kachkovs'kyi did not know that a Supreme Rusyn Council had been established in Lviv until he read a circular letter by Bishop Hryhorii Iakymovych who had recently been named bishop of Peremysl.

When Iakymovych left for his new post on 23 May 1848, he wrote a circular letter about the new situation among the Rusyns in Galicia. In this letter he recounted the events that had occurred in Lviv in the past month. Mykhailo Kachkovs'kyi first heard about them on reading that letter. He was very impressed with the program that the Rusyns had promoted, that they had the support of Count Franz Stadion (the governor of Galicia), and that they had acted in an orderly manner.[30]

Kachkovs'kyi also observed that the Polish press had been undependable. The Poles had rioted and caused grave disorder that had to be suppressed by the military, and they had openly defied the civil authorities and challenged the authority of the Austrian emperor. From that time on, Kachkovs'kyi changed from a Rusyn with Polish sympathies to a Rusyn with Russian sympathies.[31]

By the 1860s Kachkovs'kyi had become a Russian voice in the development of Rusyn literature. He read the newspaper *Zoria halytska* with its Cyrillic alphabet and he also studied Iosif Levtsko's German-Russian grammar and other new works in literary Russian. Kachkovs'kyi, for the next few decades, became a leader among the pro-Russians in the fight to Russify the Rusyn literary language. To the extent that he was political, he became a supporter of Russia and finally died on a trip to Russia and was buried there in 1872.

However, Kachkovs'kyi never converted to Russian Orthodoxy. He died a Greek Catholic and because of that his grave was virtually unmarked until 1884 when A. V. Vasilev, the president of the St. Petersburg's Slavonic Benevolent Society, visited the grave and supplied it with a white marble memorial.[32]

While this account is just the sketch of one man, it was repeated in outline form many times among the generation of Rusyn intellectuals who were adults in 1848. They became enamored of Russian culture without being unduly influenced by political agendas. They remained Greek Catholics and were led by a group of culturally pro-Russian priests in Lviv, often called "St. George's Clique."

The same cannot be said about the next generation of pro-Russian Rusyns who were young students in 1848. These men adopted the Russian heritage. Perhaps the best representative of this generation was Ioann Grigorevich Naumovich.

Ioann Naumovich was born in 1826. He experienced the typical youth of a son of a Greek Catholic priest and prepared for the priesthood himself. His studies at the Greek Catholic seminary in Lviv were interrupted by the uprising of 1848. Up to this time he, like Kachkovs'kyi and numerous other Galician Rusyn intellectuals, was strongly influenced by the Polish national spirit and culture. During the Polish uprising in Lviv in 1848, however, an interesting event occurred that taught the young Naumovich the utility of being a "Russian."[33] According to his biographer, he was standing on a hill overlooking the fighting between the Imperial soldiers and the Polish nationalists when he was arrested by the Imperial soldiers who assumed he was a Polish participant. He, however, convinced the soldiers that he was a Russian and on that basis he was released.[34]

Shortly after that incident he left Lviv and went to Verkhobuzh, east of Lviv, to tutor the children of a Father Tarnovski. There he came in contact with the Russian soldiers who, in 1849, were on their way to pacify the Hungarians. And there again the typical stereotypes were destroyed. The Russian officers were surprised to find intelligent "Russian"-speaking people in Austrian lands, and Naumovich was surprised to find that the Russians were not "drunken thieves" but were warm-hearted and well bred.

In 1850 Naumovich returned to Lviv and finished his seminary education and took the vows of priesthood in the Greek Catholic church. By that time Naumovich had become strongly pro-Russian and after his ordination, he joined the clergy's movement to "protest against bringing Latin parts into the traditional ritual of the Greek Catholic worship service."[35]

In 1872, just after the death of Mykhailo Kachkovs'kyi, Naumovich founded an enlightenment society in Kolomia, in Bukovina, in honor of Kachkovs'kyi. The main purpose of this society, according to its constitution, was to "broaden, among the Russian people of Austria, knowledge of science, love for the church's correct Holy Rite, diligence, steadfastness, charity in the home, self-awareness and integrity." In the first year the society received 5,000 members, most of whom were Galicians. In its third year, the society moved its headquarters to Lviv to be in the center of Galician Rusyn life.[36]

In May 1877, an entire village in eastern Galicia, under the influence of Naumovich, converted to Orthodoxy and sent a notice to that effect to the Uniate consistory in Lviv. It is interesting to note that while Naumovich was "Orthodox at heart," he was still a Greek Catholic priest and felt that he would be breaking his ordination vows if he were to convert to Orthodoxy. However, in the months that followed, the entire district of Gnilichka converted to Orthodoxy under the leadership of Naumovich. This scandal in the Greek Catholic church led to the resignation of Joseph Sembratovich, the metropolitan responsible for the Rusyns in Galicia.[37]

After these events, Naumovich was not to go unpunished and in January 1881, he was arrested by the Galician authorities and charged with treason. It must be pointed out that the arrest was not for converting a district to Orthodoxy, but for Naumovich's Russian connections, which the authorities chose to interpret as political rather than cultural or religious. The prosecution successfully linked Naumovich and the other defendants with the Slavic Benevolent Society in St. Petersburg and with several official Russian channels in Vienna.[38] The prosecution's case was probably factually correct. As early as 1867 a number of the Galician Russophile leaders had contact with the Russian Pan-Slavic societies and received money and materials from them through the chaplain of the Russian embassy in Vienna.[39]

The trial of Naumovich and his associates was prolonged and caused considerable interest and excitement in the press. It was not until July 1882, that he was finally convicted and sentenced to eight months in jail. After his jail term, Naumovich sent a petition to the pope asking to be released from his ordination vows. The pope never responded to this request and finally on 6 October 1885, Naumovich formally "returned" to Orthodoxy in a ceremony in the Orthodox church in Lviv.[40]

After his imprisonment, however, life in Galicia became increasingly difficult for him. He emigrated to Russia, but closely followed the pro-Russian movement in Galicia. The arrest of Naumovich and the other leaders of the pro-Russian group called the "St. George clique" marked the decline of the pro-Russian movement as a leading group among the Rusyns in Galicia.[41]

In Subcarpathia, the Rusyn intellectual leaders were also political conservatives. Their two most outstanding leaders were Aleksander Dukhnovych and Ivan I. Rakovs'kyi. In cultural and linguistic matters they were even more actively pro-Russian than their counterparts in Galicia. They were most active in developing a Rusyn-Russian cultural identity for their people and in developing a literary language to supplement that identity.

Rakovs'kyi was a pastor and a publicist, Aleksander Dukhnovych, a pastor and an educator. Both of them were successful in developing the Rusyn-Russian language and encouraging its use. Both of them felt that the vernacular Rusyn was an inferior language and tried to adapt literary Russian to the uses of the Rusyns.[42] They were successful in opening new Rusyn schools, publishing pro-Rusyn-Russian books, and encouraging the priesthood to upgrade their language in their sermons. To a far greater degree than in Galicia, the Subcarpathian Rusyn intellectuals were able to convince the Rusyn people that they were closely akin to the Great Russians and that their literary and cultural future lay in association with the Great Russians. Partially because of their success, there was no significant populist Ukrainian movement among the intellectuals in Subcarpathia as developed in Galicia.[43]

Throughout the decade of the 1850s, the intellectual leaders in Subcarpathia were in contact with the leaders of Galicia. The Subcarpathian leaders were strong advocates of a union of Subcarpathia and Galicia. But the correspondence and the articles published by both parties in *Zoria halitskya*, the Galician journal published in Lviv, indicated that the two groups of Rusyn intellectuals would not have been able to agree on a common cultural development.[44]

For several decades after 1848 the Galician Rusyns had three cultural-national choices rather than two. In addition to the "All-Russian" and "Ukrainian" concepts, they could have chosen the "Rusyn" concept advocated, in some form, by Subcarpathian intellectuals such as Aleksander Dukhnovych. In the 1850s he was a canon in the Prešov eparchy of the Greek Catholic church. He was responsible for education in the diocese and used his position to combine the Rusyn pride and consciousness with the Russian ideal. Dukhnovych introduced literary Russian into the gymnasium in Prešov and even taught other classes in literary Russian. Since he was a popular teacher, his upgrading of the "people's" language was tolerated and even accepted.[45] He also founded the Prešov Literary Society.[46] He was instrumental in founding the St. Basil Society in Uzhhorod and was a major contributor to many slavic journals.[47]

Dukhnovych advocated uniting the Rusyn people in Galicia and Subcarpathia into a single crown land with self-government under the Austrian emperor. This would free the Rusyns from cultural dominance by the Poles and Hungarians. Dukhnovych's program would have limited the concept of Rusyn national identity to the Rusyns in the Austrian Empire. Such a limitation was not consistent with the Ukrainian idea and certainly not a Russian idea. Regarding the language issue, Dukhnovych was against elevating a dialect to a literary language. While he probably thought the vernacular was inadequate as a basis for a literary language, his primary argument against it was the "absurd thought that 40 million [sic] Rusyns [Slavs?] in the Austrian Empire should adopt 1 of 1,000 dialects as their literary language."[48]

By 1852, an article was published in Zoria halytska entitled, "Our Aspirations Regarding the Formation of our Language."[49] While this article did not yet advocate a Ukrainian dialect over any other dialect, it did suggest in persuasive terms that Church Slavonic was not an acceptable language and that a more popular literary language would be necessary to unite the people with their literature. From that time on, Zoria halytska policy actually favored the development of a dialect as the solution to the literary language problem. This approach by the more populist Rusyn intellectuals in Galicia created a rift between the church-centered conservatives and the developing group of populist intellectuals who became identified with the Ukrainian movement in the 1860s and 1870s.

This populist movement had far-reaching implications for the cultural development of the Rusyn people in the next decades. The populists were unable to take over the institutions controlled by the conservatives so they started new organizations. These populists had little effect on the intellectual movement in Subcarpathia. As a result, the conservative institutions in Lviv and the intellectual organizations in Subcarpathia were essentially cut off from the populist movements.

With the populist viewpoint missing, the conservative groups became even more Pro-Russian, linguistically but not necessarily politically.[50] In the mid-1850s, Ivan Rakovs'kyi, a Subcarpathian, was the most ardent and persuasive Russophile. By 1856 he had become convinced that the Rusyns were ethnically one with the Great Russians and he began advocating Russian as the literary language of the Rusyns. As far as he was concerned the Rusyns should even alter their pronunciation to conform to the Great Russian language.[51]

In 1856 Rakovs'kyi began publishing Tserkovnaia gazeta in literary Russian. This publication was suspended in 1857 by the Austrian government's ban on publication in nonofficial languages. The following year he began to publish Tserkovnyi viestnik in Church Slavonic to get around the ban.[52] During the next few decades a number of newspapers and journals were published in Subcarpathia in literary Russian. They all met with

varying degrees of failure, sometimes because of government
policy and sometimes because they lacked extensive circulation.

These earlier efforts in both Galicia and Subcarpathia to identify Rusyn culture with Great Russian culture were primarily
indigenous attempts. There is no evidence that Russian propaganda played a significant role in its genesis other than the
significant but indirect role played by the Russian occupation of
Hungary.

In the 1860s and 1870s, however, the situation changed considerably. The conservative church-oriented Rusyn leaders were
eclipsed in both Galicia and Subcarpathia. In Subcarpathia, the
Magyarization policy successfully suppressed most Rusyn nationalist movements. In Galicia the populist Ukrainian movement became the more vibrant force and by the end of the
century the radical Ukrainian movement began to dominate the
Galician intellectual and popular scene. Finally, the Russian
cultural movement gained direct support from Russia and became a Russian movement rather than a Rusyn movement. As a
result of these changes, the Rusyn national idea was all but
obliterated by the turn of the century. The Rusyn intellectuals
who refused to be absorbed by Polish or Hungarian culture generally limited themselves to two options: they became Ukrainians
or Russophiles.[53]

In Galicia the Ukrainian movement was perhaps "born" of the
National-Populist movement that developed in the 1870s. This
Nationalist-Populist movement was led by priests who wished to
influence the peasants by establishing reading rooms in the villages. These reading rooms were often associated with the local
pastor and the local parish. Father Stepan Kachala was a leading
figure in this movement. He was most famous for his booklet
against drinking and laziness among the peasants. His booklet
"What is Destroying Us and What Can Help Us?" placed the
responsibility for the peasants' plight on the peasants' own behavior. Father Kachala suggested a "Horatio Alger" approach to
improving the condition of a whole class of exploited people.[54]

During the 1880s a new group of leaders wrested control of the
Ukrainian movement from the priests. Several of these leaders
were peasants themselves and they recognized the systemic factors of poverty among the peasants. They resented the clergy as
representatives of the elite. This new generation of leaders, however, built on the foundations laid by the priests as they gradually
turned the reading rooms in the villages into centers for their
own national and social ideas.[55]

If the decades of the 1850s and 1860s belonged to the "Old Ruthenians" and Russophiles, and the 1880s belonged to national populists, the decades at the turn of the century belonged to the radical Ukrainians who by 1890 had organized the Ukrainian Radical party.[56] Its most significant leaders were Ivan Franko, Michael Pavlyk, and Iuliian Bachyns'kyi.

These young radicals were socialists and they were able to develop a specific economic and political program. They were anticlerical and they had a program for redistributing the wealth and aiding the peasants. Politically, they advocated full independence for the Ukrainians from the Austrian Empire. They were also the first Galician Ukrainians to work actively with the eastern Ukrainians under Russia, and when Russia suppressed Ukrainian activity in the East, these radicals served as hosts transferring the center of Ukrainian activity from Kiev to Lviv.[57]

The Ukrainian movement, while populist in ideology, was still a movement of the intellectuals until the mid-1890s. So while the Ukrainian movement developed into a full-fledged popular movement among the Galician Rusyns after the turn of the century, that movement had not affected the earlier peasant immigrants to the United States where a large number of the immigrants converted to Orthodoxy and identified themselves as Russians.

The Subcarpathian Rusyns came to the United States with a cultural identity focused on the Greek Catholic church. In Subcarpathia, the Magyarization effort was in full force in the 1880s. The Greek Catholic bishops were appointed only from the thoroughly Magyarized priesthood. The bishops in turn tried to encourage the priests to Magyarize the people. This pressure was so direct that it alienated people from the clergy.[58] When these peasants from Subcarpathia came to the United States, their primary concern was to save the Greek Catholic church as a Rusyn institution. In the United States, while many Subcarpathian congregations did join the Orthodox church, a significant number remained Greek Catholic but identified themselves as Russians and resisted the efforts of the Ukrainian movement.

It is apparent that Russian culture had a strong influence on the Rusyns in both Galicia and Subcarpathia in the last half of the nineteenth century. In the earlier part of this period, Russia was not an active contributor to the Rusyn intellectuals' search for self-identity. The Rusyns seemed to be oppressed by the Hungarians, the Poles, and even the Austrians. In 1849, when the

Russian troops occupied Hungary, the Rusyns found a natural affinity with them that contributed to the development of a pro-Russian movement in both Galicia and Subcarpathia.

This Russian affinity had an impact on the Rusyn intellectuals' search for a national identity. In the decade of the 1840s and early 1850s, the Rusyn intellectuals had viewed themselves as a nationality within the Austrian Empire. This view excluded both the Great Russian concept and, in its political form, the Ukrainian concept. With the expanded consciousness that resulted from the events of 1848 and 1849, both those concepts became possible. In the 1850s and 1860s the pro-Russian concept of national identity was a viable option among Rusyn intellectuals in both Galicia and Subcarpathia.

The Russian idea was ultimately eclipsed by the Ukrainian idea in Galicia if not in Subcarpathia.[59] Lost causes such as that of the Russians' cultural efforts with the Rusyns are generally underrepresented in historical research, but the Russian cause was important while it was an option for the Rusyns. It is also important to note that the Rusyn peasants in eastern Galicia did not become anti-Russian just because they became Ukrainian.

Apparently Andrei Sheptyts'kyi, who was metropolitan of Lviv prior to World War I, also maintained a balanced position between the views of the Russophiles and the Ukrainian national movement. He was never interested in rejecting the Russian Orthodox East in favor of the Catholic West since he felt his Greek Catholic church could be a bridge between the two.[60] While intellectuals may draw hard lines between competing cultural perceptions, the people may not be so exclusive in their allegiances.

Finally in the 1880s, the Ukrainian idea with its populist and radical viewpoints became the majority view in Galicia while national identity among the Rusyn intellectuals in Subcarpathia was largely stifled by Magyarization.

In the 1870s and 1880s the influence of the Pan-Slavic movements in Russia peaked and the pattern of interest changed. The Rusyns had to search for Russian culture in the 1850s. From the 1870s until the First World War, the pattern was reversed. The Russian Slavic associations provided the Rusyns with organizations for cultural heritage and cultural exchange in both Europe and America.

2

Russian Interests in the Rusyns in the Austro-Hungarian Empire from 1900 to World War I

The relationship between Russia and the Slavs of the Austrian Empire in the late nineteenth and early twentieth centuries has often been discussed as a period of Russian Pan-Slavism. This Pan-Slavism has often been equated with Russian imperialism, but in the case of the Rusyns some modifications need to be made in this classical interpretation.[1]

Many accounts of Pan-Slavism mark the end of active Pan-Slavism with the Russo-Turkish war, which culminated with the Congress of Berlin in 1878.[2] It is probably more correct to suggest that Pan-Slavism continued to remain active albeit in a slightly modified form. It lost its overtly political and military aspects but continued as a religious and cultural force.[3]

Konstantin Pobedonostsev was a significant figure in this modified Pan-Slavic policy at the turn of the century. Pobedonostsev was an advisor to Tsar Nicholas II and procurator of the Holy Synod (secular administrator of the Russian Orthodox church). Pobedonostsev has been identified as an isolationist except for a short period in 1877−78 when he seemed excited with the Pan-Slavic doctrine.[4] Yet in the period following 1878, "Pobedonostsev used the Russian Orthodox church abroad in an aggressive effort to promote Russian culture and the interests of the secular Russian state."[5]

After 1878 Pobedonostsev developed a policy of promoting knowledge of Balkan culture in Russia and promoting knowledge of Russian Orthodoxy in the Balkans and Eastern Europe.[6] Pobedonostsev promoted a kind of "cultural imperialism" waged by churchmen and scholars with the knowledge and support of the Ministry of Foreign Affairs.[7] Russia, under the guidance of Pobedonostsev, also extended her cultural imperialism to the United States during the same period.

Pobedonostsev "was particularly eager to convert Uniates who had emigrated from Galicia to cities such as Pittsburgh and Chicago, in part because this might assist his campaign among the Uniates in Galicia, the Carpatho-Ukraine [Subcarpathia], and Russia itself."[8] Pan-Slavism had taken on the form of "cultural imperialism."

Cultural imperialism should not be interpreted as a policy of forced Russian expansion. There was a certain mutuality to the interactions between the Rusyns and the Russians. Much of the interest between Rusyns and Russians had been initiated by the Rusyns.[9] Neither was Pan-Slavism a singular tool of Russian imperialism.[10] Many of the "captive Slavs" in the Austrian Empire as well as in the Ottoman Empire looked to Russia for a cultural identity as well as political salvation.

In the decade prior to the outbreak of the First World War, the Russian government actively encouraged cultural and political activities that would draw the Rusyns and the Russians closer together. In doing so they were building on associations that had developed on an unofficial level in the earlier decades.[11]

The Russian Pan-Slavs supported the Serbian nationalists in Serbia because Serbian nationalism was compatible with Russia's objectives for that area.[12] The Russian Pan-Slavs did not support the local nationalism in Galicia. In Galicia the local nationalism, the Ukrainian movement, was not compatible with Russia's objectives for that area. The Russian cultural endeavor in Galicia and Subcarpathia was directed toward the cultural assimilation of the Rusyns into the Great Russian population.

The conflict between the "Muskophiles" and the Ukrainians in Galicia must be understood in the context of the political atmosphere that existed in Galicia at the time. The year 1890 introduced a new period in Galician politics referred to as the "new era" during which efforts were made to attain a Polish-Ukrainian compromise.[13]

The reason for this new era can be traced to Vienna. The Austrian minister of foreign affairs, Count Gustav Kálnoky, recognized the growing tension between Austria and Russia. He also recognized the potential for Russia to take advantage of the oppression of the Rusyns by the Poles in Galicia. The Ukrainian movement was developing as an effective counterforce to the pro-Russian movement. As a result, he encouraged the Polish leaders in Galicia to accommodate the Ukrainian movement and grant them some concessions.

The Poles seemed inclined to support that position until the

Ukrainians also demanded political equality. This demand the Poles refused to grant and the cooperation ended with the elections of 1895 when the Poles manipulated the election laws in their favor.[14]

The Imperial government in Vienna, however, continued to recognize the importance of supporting the Ukrainian movement; that government aided the Ukrainians in gaining more privileges from the Poles. Election reforms, which became effective in January 1907, gave the Rusyns a larger share of the delegate seats in the Reichsrat. The reform was not perfect, however, since it still required 102,000 Rusyns per seat in the Reichsrat, while the Poles received a delegate for every 52,000 inhabitants.[15]

That election in 1907 also demonstrated that the Ukrainian movement was becoming the popular force among the Rusyn population at the expense of the pro-Russian faction. Of the twenty-seven Rusyn delegates elected to the Reichsrat, twenty-two were Ukrainians and only five were pro-Russian. In the 1913 elections to the Diet the pro-Russians won only one seat while the Ukrainians won thirty-one seats.[16]

In 1904 a pro-Russian writer, Vladimir Shchavinskii, analyzed the cultural competition in Galicia between the pro-Russian faction and the Ukrainians.[17] He noticed that the revival of "Little Russian" (Ukrainian) literature in the eastern Ukraine (inside Russia) could not continue without influencing the Galician Rus'. Shchavinskii argued that the Ukrainian movement was encouraged by the Poles and the Austrians who were threatened by the development of "Russian national thought" among the Rusyns. Shchavinskii also suggested that the great leaders of the Russian movement, Adol'f Dobrians'kyi and Father Ioann Naumovich, had advocated the union of the "Little Russian" people with the people of Great Russia.[18]

Shchavinskii reflected the position of the Russophile group regarding Russian interests in Galicia. He argued that the Rusyn people were Russians, mostly peasants and largely illiterate. These people needed to be educated in their literary language, which was Russian, and to be taught that they were one with the Great Russian people.

Against this Russian position The Ukrainians could appeal to the Rusyns arguing that they were not uncultured; they had a culture that was different from the Russian culture. They spoke their own literary language, subject only to a standardization of the various dialects. They had been kept illiterate by the Poles, but learning to read their own language would emphasize their own identity and be a source of pride for them.

Vladimir Shchavinskii did not admit the success of the Ukrainian movement, but he offered a series of statistics that supported that fact. His first set of statistics are not conclusive. There were two major societies among the Rusyns. The Russian society was named for Mykhailo Kachkovs'kyi and the Ukrainian society was called the Prosvita (Enlightenment) Society. The Kachkovs'kyi Society sponsored almost one thousand reading rooms throughout Galicia, while the Prosvita sponsored thirteen hundred reading rooms. In the seven seminaries for the Rusyn population, 250 students were of the Russian party while 700 were of the Ukrainian party. The Russians published one daily newspaper, four biweekly and two monthly newspapers, and two journals. The Ukrainians published three dailies, five weeklies, eight biweeklies, nine monthlies, and one literary journal.

Each had a scientific society. The Russian one was called the Galician-Russian Matitsa and the Ukrainians' was called the Shevchenko Scientific Society. In the Russian public library called Narodny Dom (National Home) there were 2,224 library visitors during the period from 1 September 1903 to 31 January 1904. During the same period, the Shevchenko Library had 2,459 readers.[19]

These statistics from a Russophile source indicate that the Ukrainians were a larger group than the Russians, but they would not necessarily suggest the overwhelming superiority of the Ukrainians over the Russians that the previously described election returns suggested.

Shchavinskii also offered some financial statistics for the two competing factions, and these statistics do indicate the decisive vitality of the Ukrainian movement over the Russian movement. The Russian party had a National Home worth 940,000 crowns with an endowment fund worth 658,000 crowns. Its Stavropigian Institute was worth 700,000 crowns with an endowment of 128,000 crowns. The Russian party's Kachkovs'kyi Society and the Galician-Russian Matitsa property was worth 250,000 crowns. The Russian party owned property with a combined total value of 3 million crowns, but it had an annual budget of only 1.5 million crowns.[20] This budget covered the costs of the publishing ventures, maintaining the home and library, and all kinds of other public relations activities in the competition with the Ukrainians.

In contrast the Ukrainian party's combined property values

totaled only 1,175,000 crowns, about one-third of the value of the Russian property. But the Ukrainian party had an operating budget of 24 million crowns, more than 13 times the annual budget for the Russian party.[21]

These figures suggest that the Ukrainian party was more vital than the Russian one especially by 1903, the year covered in the statistics. Much of the money collected in Russia for the Russophile party in Galicia probably went into the purchase and maintenance of large and attractive buildings. The Ukrainian party, on the other hand, had a more limited capital investment, but evidently had a larger circulation for its publications. They could turn the proceeds from the sale of their publications back into the production of new materials several times a year. Thus they could operate as large a budget as they did with a much smaller capital investment.

As a general rule, it was possible for both the Ukrainians and the Russophiles to propagate their views among the Rusyn population. There was always the Polish opposition, but since Vienna insisted that the Ukrainian party be encouraged at the expense of the Russian party, the Poles were not free to suppress nationalistic activity among the Rusyns.

The Polish government of Galicia did, however, regulate the competition between the Ukrainians and the Russophiles in what seemed to be an effort to keep them divided. For example, in 1902, the government revoked the license for the Stavropigian Institute to publish in the Rusyn dialect. This decision limited the Stavropigian's influence to those who could read Russian. At the same time it significantly increased the business for the competing Shevchenko Society press.[22]

While the Austrian government did not suppress the national movements, not even the Russophile movement, among the Rusyns in Galicia for fear that the suppression would play into Russia's hand, the Hungarians made every effort to suppress the Russophile movement among the Rusyns in northern Hungary. Occasionally the Magyars found it necessary to provide support for the Rusyn language as a means of undercutting the Russophile movement. They supported the Rusyn newspaper *Karpat* from 1872 to 1886 but it was a rather sterile project and limited to government news in its coverage. For the most part, the Magyarones among the Rusyns, led by Istvan Pankovics, the Greek Catholic bishop of Munkachevo, did their best to limit any Rusyn autonomy.[23]

A correspondent to *Slavianskii viek* (The Slavic Age) in 1903 reported that a Rusyn priest wrote to his bishop, John Valyi, (Rusyn Greek Catholic bishop of Prešov) in the Rusyn dialect. Bishop Valyi promptly wrote back that the Rusyn priests were to correspond with him only in an official language, either Latin or Hungarian, not in "Rutenskom."[24] The use of an "official language" was part of a Magyar campaign to ban the use of Rusyn as a language of correspondence and old Slavonic as a liturgical language. By the turn of the century the Hungarian government no longer encouraged the use of the Rusyn dialect even as a means to counteract Russian influence.

The use of the Russian language was discouraged but the journal, *Slavianskii viek*, was published in Russian and achieved some underground circulation within Hungary. *Slavianskii viek* was published in Vienna from 1901 to 1904 by a Carpatho-Rusyn, Dmitri Vergun. A statement of purpose was printed on the back of several of the early issues of the journal. The statement identified *Slavianskii viek* as an "all Slav periodical published in the Russian language."

The statement further identified three objectives for the journal: It would give Russian and Slavic readers a full, clear, and honest presentation of cultural life in all Slavdom. It would begin to meet the wish of the southwestern Slavs to become acquainted with Russian speech so that the Russian language might become, in time, the chief language for intercourse between Slavs. *Slavianskii viek* would also encourage commercial intercourse between the west Slavic lands and Russia.

The statement finally concluded that the journal, as the enemy of prejudice, would endeavor to be "all Slavic in all things." It would offer every Slav the opportunity for free and candid discussion of current Slavic questions in his own language with parallel texts in Russian to give Russian readers the opportunity to become acquainted with Slavic languages and facilitate other Slavs in their study of Russian.[25]

In 1903, *Slavianskii viek* published 1,200 to 1,250 copies of each issue with a subscription list of 1,123 distributed as follows: St. Petersburg 144, Moscow 188, Odessa 39, Kiev 20, Krakow 10, Warsaw 18. In the Russian provinces and Siberia there were 305 subscribers making a total of 654 subscribers in the Russian Empire. *Slavianskii viek* had 63 subscribers in Vienna, 111 in Galicia and Bukovina, 102 in the Czech crown lands, and 60 in Slovenia and Dalmatia. The 40 subscribers in Hungary received their copies in plain, closed envelopes because the Hungarian government had suppressed its circulation there. Serbia and Bulgaria received 59, Germany 16, France 12, Switzerland 2, and America 3.[26]

These circulation statistics indicate that the journal had a wide geographical distribution. If many of the subscriptions were held by Slavic and Russian circles throughout Eastern Europe and Russia, the journal probably reached a large percentage of those interested in the Pan-Slavic idea.

The founder and editor of *Slavianskii viek*, Dmitri Vergun, fits the description of a frustrated "Austrian Slav" nationalist who looked to Russia for political, cultural, and national redemption. Vergun began his career as a Carpatho-Rusyn (Galician) poet. In the 1890s he published two volumes of his poetry in Lviv.[27] From 1901 to 1904 he edited *Slavianskii viek* in Vienna. While there he founded the "Circle of Friends of the Russian Language." This circle met regularly and discussed contemporary Russian writers such as Vasily (Basil) A. Zhukovskii, Nicholas Nekrasov, and Vladimir Soloviev. The members of the circle also discussed Russian history, geography, economics, and popular philosophical issues.[28] The circle was obviously interested in more than just the Russian language.

After his term as publisher-editor of *Slavianskii viek*, Dmitri Vergun moved to St. Petersburg where he became a lecturer for and finally vice-president of the Galician-Russian Benevolent Society.[29] This society was the key through which the Russian government directed its propaganda interests in Galicia. Its president, Count Vladimir Bobrinskii, was the brother of Count Iurii Bobrinskii who was later appointed military governor of Galicia during the Russian offensive in 1914.

The war and Russian Revolution were very difficult for Vergun. His father died in Tallerhaff, an Austrian concentration camp, and his dream for a Slavic federation under the Russian umbrella was crushed by the Communist Revolution. His feelings were best expressed in a poem he wrote for the new year 1920:

ROKOVOI GOD
(The Fateful Year)

What do you hold
For us New Year?
The olive branch of peace
Or trampling of fresh spilled blood?
Will the thunder of the executioner's axe prevail
And quiet turbulent Europe?

Will more than the scarlet-purple ruling class
Fall to the delight of rebellious serfs.
The hymn of freedom
Under the sky
Tempts us
With the universal promise
And seduces us
Offering an idyllic paradise.
Will orphan Carpathia enter into the realm of the land of his
    family's birth?
And will the Russian brothers be united in a marriage of the Volga
    and the Danube?
The future cannot be seen in the dregs.
But the voice of the prophet suggests
The fate of the Slavs will rise.
A crown to you Russia-mother.[30]

Dmitri Vergun was pro-Russian and anti-Ukrainian. In Odessa in 1918 he wrote "Russkii Flag," which reflected his thoughts "after Petliura [the Ukrainian leader] was expelled from Odessa." In the poem he suggested that the tricolor flag, the tsarist flag, was the symbol of "Freedom, Faith, Peace," but over and over he repeated that the blue and yellow [Ukrainian] was an "Austrian flag."[31]

Finally his poem "Sedina" (Grey Hair) suggested that Soviet Russia was not the Russia he had hoped would emerge. He wrote, "My 'Russland' is surviving as a putrid shambles. . . . I have lost my family, my homeland, and mother, and my father's grave is in a foreign country."[32]

World War I and the Russian Revolution did not deal kindly with the dreams of the Pan-Slavists. But in 1901 when Dmitri Vergun was a young man, Russia offered the hope for a national revival among the Rusyns in Hungary. And for four years, the journal he edited, Slavianskii viek, served as a center of communication for the Pan-Slavic movement.

Each issue of Slavianskii viek generally contained three sections. The first part contained theoretical articles designed to clarify the objectives of the "All Slav" movement and to search for a common ground of understanding among the various Slavic peoples. The second part of the journal contained correspondence from the various Slavic centers throughout Eastern Europe and Russia. The third part included literary sketches and poems designed to familiarize the readers with "Slavic" (Russian) literary styles.

The correspondence section would generally be divided into two parts. One part, often entitled "Russki kruzhki" (Russian circles), contained news from the Russian clubs located outside the Russian Empire. These clubs generally focused on increasing the members' knowledge of contemporary Russia and the Russian language. For example, on 25 February 1903, the "Russian circle" met in Prague and honored the memory of the Russian folk poet, Nicholas Nekrasov, on the twenty-fifth anniversary of his death.[33]

In May 1903, the correspondent from Lviv described the increasing activity of the Russian society there.[34] In September 1902, the society sponsored a meeting of "Russian" (Rusyn) students in Austria-Hungary. In February 1903, there was a meeting of Russian (Rusyn) men from throughout "Chervonaia Rus'" (Galicia). At the same time there was an organizational meeting of Russian journalists in Lviv. On 12 March there was a meeting of Russian (Rusyn) women. The correspondent, I. Svintsov, observed that this display of life in the Russian society in that "oppressed and forgotten corner of the Russian land" suggested the striving of those people to participate in the cultural and spiritual life of the Russian people.

All the writers contributing to *Slavianskii viek* used the term *Russian* rather than *Rusyn* when referring to the people of eastern Galicia and northern Hungary. For the other Slavic peoples, however, they continued to use their national names such as Czech, Pole, Serb, Bulgarian, or Croatian. This pattern suggests that the "All Slavists" represented by *Slavianskii viek* consistently thought of eastern Galicia and northern Hungary as being "Russian."

There was very little correspondence from the Rusyns in northern Hungary. When an occasional letter appeared entitled "Iz Ugrorossii" (from Hungarian Rus'), the author was always anonymous.[35]

The correspondence section would occasionally contain routine news from the Slavs who emigrated to the United States. On one occasion it reported on a convention of Slavic journalists in St. Louis that was attended by Victor Gladik, the editor of the Galician immigrant paper *Pravda*, and Paul Zhatkovich, the editor of *Amerikansky Russky Viestnik*, as well as other Slavic writers.[36]

Some of the more significant reports from the United States in 1904 described the effort to solidify support for Russia in the Russo-Japanese war. This effort was supported by several immigrant newspaper editors including Victor Gladik of *Pravda* and Father Benedict Turkevich of *Svit*. *Pravda* was published by the Russian Brotherhood Organization and *Svit* was the official organ of a Russian Orthodox Mutual Aid Society.[37] It is interesting to note that the leading newspaper for the Rusyns from northern Hungary, *Amerikansky Russky Viestnik*, did not participate in this Russophile effort.

In another letter, Michael Pupin, a Serb who was at that time a professor at Columbia University, wrote of his attempts to create pro-Russian sympathy among the general public in New York. He had written a brochure entitled, "Working Men Watch the War" (The Russo-Japanese War of 1904). From his description of its contents, Mr. Pupin was appealing to anti-Asian sentiments in the United States. He described Russia as a hero of the working class, conquering for the benefit of the working class the "yellow enemy" who would steal the jobs from American workers. Mr. Pupin personally distributed this pamphlet to the major newspapers in New York and was satisfied with the printed response of most of the newspapers.[38]

Mr. Pupin also reported a pro-Russian meeting held in New York that was attended by the Russian consul general, I. N. Ladiienskii, who, in the name of Russia, thanked those attending for their support for Russia.[39]

This correspondence from America demonstrated that Russia placed value on propaganda among the Slavic as well as non-Slavic people in America for a Russian war that was of some concern to the American government but scarcely of any concern to the average American.

Correspondence in *Slavianskii viek* from the Slavic societies within Russia indicated considerably different interests on the part of the Russian "All Slavists." The Slavic Society in Warsaw heard a lecture by a Professor Zigel on the "decline of the western Slavs." The western Slavs—Poles, Czechs, and Baltic Slavs (He identified the Balts as Slavs)—declined because they had yielded to western influence and they had accepted the civilization and Christianity of the West.[40]

The Slavic societies in St. Petersburg were more often concerned with Russia's destiny. When they contemplated the destiny of Russia, they remembered the recent past when the 1878 treaty of San Stefano had given Russia much of her objectives in the Balkans. But in subsequent negotiations at Berlin, the Western powers deprived Russia of most of that victory. Count N. P.

Ignatiev, one of the negotiators of the treaty of San Stefano, was one of the favorite speakers at the various Slavic society meetings throughout the major Russian cities. In 1903, Count Ignatiev was elected president of the Slavic Benevolent Society.[41]

In his speech to that society Count Ignatiev described his understanding of the nature of the Slavic Society. He said that the critics of Pan-Slavism argue that the Pan-Slavic societies are just like the Pan-German societies. Both work for the domination of Europe. Ignatiev responded that the society was not engaged in politics. The society sought only to help the Slavs who look to Russia for enlightenment.[42]

Ignatiev continued:

> I have unwavering faith in the fulfillment of the Great Russian idea, that if 134 million Russian people are to reach the Fatherland, it is necessary to overcome the many enemies that seek to divide the people, and clear the atmosphere of everyone who is now unfavorable to us. . . . Our society must not give up hope, but must serve everyone as examples of patriotism and not give up the ideals of our forerunners, the great strugglers for Slavdom, and persistently strive to draw together into a union all Slavdom and Russia, but without persistent effort nothing will be accomplished.[43]

Ignatiev probably represented the Russian concept of Pan-Slavism. He used the term "Great Russian Idea" while Vergun referred to the "Great Slavic Idea." Ignatiev was never specific as to exactly who should be included in the "Great Russian Idea" but one is left with the impression that the "Great Russian Idea" was perhaps greater than the "Great Slavic Idea."

Ignatiev argued that his concept of Pan-Slavism was not similar to Pan-Germanism because his "Idea" was not political. Indeed he did place his emphasis on "enlightenment" rather than military force. Enlightenment could possibly persuade the Slavs to join Russia, but it could hardly convince Germany, Austria, Hungary, and Turkey to surrender control of territory occupied by Slavs. The Pan-German and Pan-Slavic ideas may not have been too dissimilar.

In general, the Russian view of Pan-Slavism was based on "natural law," with the objective that Russian leadership should free the Slavs from domination by non-Slavic peoples and in some manner unite them under Russian protection. Natural law can be very useful in argumentation. One contributor to *Sla-*

vianskii viek argued that it was superficial to suggest that Russia won the right to intervene in the Ottoman Empire on behalf of the Christians in 1774 (Treaty of Kuchuk-Kainarji) and lost that right in 1856 (Treaty of Paris ending the Crimean War). Such laws are human laws. Russia's claim was based on natural law and was revealed through the consciousness of man. The statement of that law existed in the living consciousness of the masses of people in the Balkans. That law will exist in their consciousness until the last person from the oppressed area will throw off his fetters and the cross is raised over the parish church instead of the crescent.[44]

This theoretical view of the Russian people and their inner guidance system was given a direct practical application by a high official in the Russian government who wrote in *Slavianskii viek* under the pen name Russkii Skif' (Russian Scythian). He bemoaned the fact that the "democratic" countries of Western Europe called Russia "barbarian." Yet it was those countries who allowed the Turks to "massacre" Armenians and Macedonians. "For centuries the Russians have advocated freedom for Serbia, Montenegro, Rumania, and Bulgaria," while "democratic" France and other Western European countries have sided with the barbarian—Turkey. He analyzed European foreign policy in the following manner:

> The Russians do not play games with words. We are people of actions. We Russians do not like to force our way of doing things on others. We do not wish to have the west interfere in Slavic affairs.
>
> We challenge the French and Italian "democrats" to back up their words with actions. To free Macedonia would require a war with Turkey. Such a war will require an army of 600,000 men and an expenditure of 3 to 4 million francs. The objectives would be great, the oppressed would be freed, the small democratic governments—Serbia, Montenegro, and Bulgaria—would be strengthened and reenforced, and the barbarians will be driven from Europe.
>
> Such a resolution of the "eastern question" the Russian people will sign with both hands. But after a victory with the Turks, would the French and Italian democracies allow independence to *all* the Balkan peoples without any thought of compensation? That would be the measure of democracy of the great powers in the West. *Then we would see that their words do not fit their actions.*[45]

This Russian official, whom Vergun identified as a "very high-placed diplomat," described a diplomatic program that reflected Slavophile and Pan-Slavic thought. First of all he stated that the

Russians did "not like to force their way of doing things on others" and the Russians did "not wish to have the west interfere in Slavic affairs." These sentiments were at the heart of the Slavophile idea. Secondly, he suggested that if the West would allow it, "the Russian people will sign with both hands" an endorsement of war against Turkey to free the Balkan Slavs. This objective fit nicely with the Pan-Slavic assumption that the Slavs would naturally gravitate toward Russia.

The Pan-Slavic contributors to *Slavianskii viek* were never explicit as to what form a final union of all Slavic peoples would take. They generally did talk about uniting with the fatherland (Ignatiev used the term *fatherland*) and did seem to infer a fairly close union.

The Slavs outside of Russia had a very different idea of Pan-Slavism. One of their most articulate spokesmen for this period was Dmitri Vergun, the editor of *Slavianskii viek*. Vergun suggested the movement adopt a new identifying slogan; he suggested "The Great Slavic Idea." Vergun did not demand consistency; he argued for practicality. The various Slavic nations could develop their own systems. A democratic Macedonia, Bulgaria, or Serbia would be perfectly compatible with an autocratic Russia. The one thing he could not accept was capitalism. He observed the capitalistic oppression of the "worker and the peasant" in the West and he could not accept it.[46]

Vergun's program was a practical one designed to gain as widespread support as possible within the Slavic community. It did not, however, please the Slavophiles in Russia as indicated by an article that Vergun received and published from a "young writer on the neo-Slavophile newspaper, the St. Petersburg *Vedomostii.*"[47] The writer argued that no form of Slavic unity would be possible without the total cooperation of Russia. Therefore, the resulting union must be centered on Russia. There could be some type of federation, but federal states must look to Russia for guidance.[48] In effect there would be no room for the developing nationalisms among the Slavs in Eastern Europe.

Dmitri Vergun had a larger historical and global context for his Pan-Slavism. He argued that the next historical period was the age of "pan-ideas." The Germans were developing the Pan-Germanic idea; the Spanish-American War turned attention to the Monroe Doctrine and Pan-Americanism. The Boer War with Britain was fought for Pan-Anglicanism and the Boxer Rebellion for Pan-Mongolism. The Coronation Festival in Delhi called attention to Pan-Indianism. There was a Pan-Latin Congress in Rome. Vergun observed that there were also collective faith ideas developing. The concept of Pan-Islam was becoming popular. Pan-Semitism or Zionism had been developing, especially since the Dreyfus affair.[49]

Vergun evaluated the theoretical function of these movements and argued that the "pan-idea" could be a very positive movement if it developed properly.[50] If virtually all the people in the world joined a pan-movement, they could provide checks and safeguards for the ambitions of other pan groups.

Vergun noticed that it was the Germanic pan groups that were particularly predatory.[51] This Pan-German threat created the immediate rationale for Pan-Slavic organization. Because of the power of the Pan-German movement, Vergun dedicated significant space to an analysis of this German movement. He identified Bjornstjerne Bjornson as the most persuasive theoretician for the Pan-German movement, and therefore Slavdom's most dangerous enemy.[52]

Bjornstjerne Bjornson was a gentle Norwegian, political philosopher, poet, and novelist. He often has been ranked with Henrik Ibsen as one of Norway's greatest writers.

Vergun charged that Bjornson advocated an association of all Germanic people, not just the Germans in Eastern Europe, but of all Germanic people including the Scandinavians, Swiss, Belgians, Hollanders, English, and Americans.

Vergun recognized that Bjornson envisioned this all-German association as a peaceful movement cooperating with the other ethnic groups in the world; but, said Vergun, that is just not the way it would work in reality. The Germans have objectives that are in direct competition with the interests of other peoples. Their aggressive interests could be achieved only at the expense of the Slavs in Eastern Europe. Any Pan-German federation would use its additional power to achieve those objectives at the expense of the Slavs.[53]

Bjornson was not an enemy of the Slavs; he in no way sanctioned an imperialistic Germany. He dreamed of a type of Pan-Germanism that would support a peaceful world. He did, however, expect German to be the common language among nations in Eastern Europe much as Vergun expected Russian to be the common language among the various Slavic peoples.[54]

Dmitri Vergun did not seem to be aware that Bjornstjerne Bjornson was sympathetic to Pan-Slavism. There was a competitor to both Pan-Slavism and Pan-Germanism that Bjornson was especially hostile to: "Great Magyaria." Bjornson wrote:

> Magyar chauvinists regard Pan-Slavism as a mirage through which they can sail on their course toward a Great Magyaria but this will be their undoing. For Pan-Slavism is a natural force with historical roots in ancient soil, a common language and powerful allies: But what is Great Magyaria? Great Magyaria has never existed.[55]

Vergun's *Slavianskii viek* ceased publication at the end of 1904, but during its four years of publication it served as a valuable communication link uniting most of the Slavic and Russian clubs inside and outside of the Russian Empire. In its theoretical articles it pointed out the different theoretical concepts that divided the clubs inside Russia from those in the Austrian Empire. Most of these clubs or societies, however, had little potential for action and most of them never organized branches that crossed imperial borders.

There was one notable exception to that rule, however, the *Galitsko-russkoe Blagotvoritel'noe Obshchestvo* (The Galician-Russian Benevolent Society). This society was founded in 1903 in St. Petersburg. It had good organizational connections in Galicia; its membership included the most powerful men and women in Russia. It was this organization that Dmitri Vergun joined in 1905, when he closed the offices of *Slavianskii viek*. During the period before World War I, he was to become that society's vice-president and most popular lecturer.[56]

In 1903 a letter in *Slavianskii viek* reported that on 9 February 1903, the Galician-Russian Benevolent Society was founded. The society was meeting in the facilities of the Russian Association in St. Petersburg.[57] There were two speakers at that opening meeting. One was Father Petrov, a poetic orator, who could "speak and say nothing." He likened the world to an artist's palette or a musician's instrument. God was that artist or musician. The nationalities of the world were like colors on the palette or strings on the instrument. If some of the colors or strings are missing, the painting or music will be incomplete and that is a crime against the spirit.

This crime against the spirit occurs when a culture allows itself to become divided. The separation of the people of Galicia and Carpatho-Russia (Subcarpathia) from the Russian nation was just such a crime. It is the obligation of a national culture to unite its people into a united nation.[58] In other words, the orator was suggesting that it was the obligation of Russia to unite in a single nation all people with a Russian culture. He included the Galicians and Subcarpathians among the people with a Russian culture.

The new president of the society, A. S. Budilovich, gave a more factually oriented speech. He said that history did not record a time when the Chervonaia Rus' (Rus' in Galicia) were not culturally and ethnically in the Russian family. For 2,000 years the Carpathians have been the "holy mountains" of the Russian family. These Chervonaia Rus' have resisted every effort of their enemies (Tartars, Magyars, Poles, Germans, and Jews) to destroy their faith (Orthodox), but in recent centuries their religious and literary ties with Russia have been strengthened.

There has been a great effort to Polonize Galicia, Germanize Bukovina, and Magyarize "Ugro-Russia." "They themselves have changed the name of the people from Russki to Ruthenian." Budilovich then gave a short sketch of the "enemies'" efforts to break the bonds that unite the Russians in Austria with the Russians in Russia. He said that the enemy was suggesting that the "Little Russians" were different from the Russians. (In other words, they were Ukrainians, not Russians.) Budilovich pointed out that it would be the official intention of the Galician-Russian Society to "counter this foreign separatist propaganda which is developing within Russia. . . . So that our interest and even our material wealth can be directed toward the Chervono-Russian area."[59]

Budilovich and his society recognized that the Ukrainian movement was the most significant opponent the Russian government had in Galicia. Virtually all the early meetings of the Galician-Russian Society attacked the problem of the Ukrainian movement. The second and third meetings of the society analyzed the philosophies of some of the Ukrainian leaders. One Ukrainian writer who was analyzed was T. A. Zinkovski whom the society decided was not a philosopher but "only an emotional student."[60]

The attack on the Ukrainian movement was a common theme in Russian publications. Tserkovnyi viestnik, the official publication of the St. Petersburg Theological Academy, regularly carried articles on Uniate-Ukrainian activities in Galicia and Subcarpathia. For example, in 1897 Tserkovnyi viestnik printed a letter from Vienna describing "church and organizational life in Galicia and Bukovina." The letter identified the Ukrainian movement and the Byzantine Catholic church as part of a single "Jesuit conspiracy." The objective of this conspiracy was to implant a "German-Austrian-Roman Catholic spirit" in the hearts of the Russian people in Galicia. The writer observed that even in patriotic hearts this spirit could be found and this conspiracy was a serious threat to the Galician spirit.[61]

These articles were very common in *Tserkovnyi viestnik* for a decade beginning in 1896, but after 1906 Galicia and the Uniate church were seldom mentioned again until 1915 when the Russian armies occupied Galicia.[62] This timing coincides with Konstantin Pobedonostsev's departure as procurator of the Holy Synod in 1905 so it is likely that he was a driving force involving the church in this Pan-Slavic endeavor.

On 3 May 1903, Dmitri Vergun was the guest lecturer at the Galician-Russian Society's meeting. He restated the argument that the Poles and Germans were trying to weaken Slavdom by creating the Ukrainian separatist movement. To support this argument he observed that the Ukrainians were already publishing a journal, *The Ruthenische Revue*, in German.[63]

From that introduction he returned to his currently favorite theme: "There is another even more dreadful force gathering against Slavdom. It is the idea of Bjornson." He then described the developing German monolith that was being created by the Pan-German movement. He concluded that if Slavdom has the will to survive, it must see the danger and it must fight and the first weapon is the Russian word (language). The Russian language, literature, papers, and journals are the most effective weapon against separatist movements like the Ukrainian movement. The second weapon must be the encouragement of self-consciousness among the oppressed Slavic peoples in the Austrian Empire. At this point Vergun excluded the Poles. He charged that they had joined a "Catholic alliance" with the Catholic Germans and were actually joined with the Germans against the Slavs.[64]

Later minutes of the society's meetings indicate that many of the leading Slavophiles, including Count Ignatiev, were also members of the society.[65] The content of the lectures of the meetings became more and more descriptive of conditions in Galicia and included census figures and pictures. An increasing number of the speakers were professional people from Galicia, such as economists, lawyers, and university professors, each describing Galicia from his perspective.[66]

On 21 December 1903, the society held a special celebration to honor the memory of St. Peter, the first metropolitan of Moscow, who was also a native of Galician Rus'. At the conclusion of the meeting, Metropolitan Flavian Gorodetskii of Kiev and Galicia was made an honorary member of the society. He accepted the honor and donated 500 rubles to the society.[67] Metropolitan Flavian was also a member of the Holy Synod, the ruling body of the Russian orthodox church.

By 1913 the membership of the society included many other names of Russia's most powerful leaders. The society did not publish a list of its members, but in 1913 the society elected a subcommittee to "aid the starving in Chervonaia Rus'." The list of the members of this committee was published in their annual proceedings for 1913 and 1914, and that list was impressive. There were sixty-eight members on that committee. The two honorary chairmen were members of the Holy Synod, the metropolitans of St. Petersburg and of Kiev. Two other members of the Holy Synod and the Synod's chief legal advisor were also on the committee. The church was represented by several other bishops including the director of the St. Petersburg Theological Academy.[68]

The government was also well represented on that committee. There were at least ten members of the state Duma represented and these were not from the minority parties, since the list included the name of N. N. L'vov, the vice-president of the Duma. There were at least five members of the Council of State (Gosudarstvenyi Sovet), and several members of the Imperial Council of Ministers (Sovet Ministra Imperatorskago Dvora). The list also included several members of the City Council of St. Petersburg.

The third bloc of representation on this Committee to Aid the Starving in Galicia came from the various Slavic societies and the newspapers. It included Count Vladimir Bobrinskii, P. D. Parensov, who was a general of infantry and the president of the Slavic Benevolent Society, and representatives from several other societies and auxiliaries. The editors of Novie vremeni, Peterburgskii listok, and Vechernie vremeni were also on the committee.

The last two groups represented were the military and the aristocracy. There were two princes and a princess on the committee. Prince Volkonskii was also a vice-president of the Duma. Princess E. V. Kantakuzin' was a maid-in-waiting to the empress and Prince Shcherbatov was a member of the Council of State. The tsar was represented by several members of his personal staff

and the military was represented by several generals and colo-
nels.[69]

The composition of that Committee to Aid the Starving in
Chervonaia Rus' was indeed impressive. Unfortunately, the annual reports of the Galician-Russian Society did not give a detailed account of that committee's activities. The annual report
for 1913 that reported the establishment of the committee did,
however, record the authority on which the committee was to
operate and the source for its operating funds.

At an executive committee meeting of the Galician-Russian
Society in October 1913, the society resolved to petition the Holy
Synod for authorization to collect donations for the starving in
Galicia. The Holy Synod responded favorably to the request and
authorized the society to solicit donations in every church under
the administration of the Synod. [70]

At the same meeting the society petitioned the Russian government's Ministry of Internal Affairs to approve that collection of
donations on behalf of the "starving Russians living in Chervonaia Rus'." This petition was also granted.[71]

This arrangement gave official authorization to the activities of
the society and very likely gave them adequate funds to carry out
their activities. The annual report also indicated that the major
newspapers gave the fund-raising effort extensive favorable
coverage.[72]

In 1913, the Galician-Russian Benevolent Society had a total
expenditure of 8,742.94 rubles. This is a surprisingly small figure
for such an ambitious organization, but the budget of the Hunger
Committee was not included in the society's budget. The two
major expenditures of the society in 1913 were 3,095.78 rubles to
aid the starving in Chervonaia Rus', and 3,373.50 rubles "for
enlightenment and other objectives."[73]

The "enlightenment" was for the benefit of the Rusyns in
Galicia. It is interesting to notice that the society spent slightly
more on enlightenment than on aid to the starving. The enlightenment money was very likely channeled through the pro-
Russian societies in Galicia to expand the reading-room system
mentioned earlier in this chapter.

The Austrian consul general in Odessa reported on the Hunger
Committee's fund-raising drive. The consul reported that in
Odessa alone 30,000 rubles were collected for the relief action
and throughout Russia on St. Nicholas Day alone, about
3,000,000 rubles were raised for the Hunger Committee.[74] These
funds caused some consternation for the Austrian and Polish

officials in Galicia, but they could find no legal basis for "police action against the Russian relief activities in Galicia and Bukovina."[75]

Perhaps the only solid link between official Russian government and unofficial activities of the Slavic societies will be found in the membership of the Hunger Committee of the Galician-Russian Benevolent Society and in its official authorization by both the Holy Synod and the Department of Internal Affairs.

While the Galician-Russian Benevolent Society could work in Galicia, that type of activity was illegal in Hungarian-controlled Subcarpathia. The Hungarian government made it very difficult for the Russians to propagandize actively in northern Hungary. Much of the propagandizing there had to be done by clandestine leafleting and most of that was done in the form of encouraging the Rusyn Uniates there to convert to Orthodoxy.

In the period from 1912 to 1914 a large number of pamphlets were circulating in the Austro-Hungarian Empire. These pamphlets were written for the purpose of convincing the Slavic population who were members of the Greek Catholic or Uniate church that they should "return to Orthodoxy." These pamphlets could circulate with some degree of freedom in the Austrian part of the empire, but within Hungary they were flatly forbidden and circulated only clandestinely.

The most interesting of these pamphlets was written by a Russian monk, Denasii, who lived in the Panteleimon Monastery on Mt. Athos in Greece.[76] The first of his pamphlets, *A Circular Letter from Athos to the Orthodox Christians*, was ostensibly directed at the Orthodox in Serbia, but it circulated far beyond that. Its content was directed as an attack on the Unia, which had created the Greek Catholic church in union with Rome. The main part of the *Circular Letter* was a reprint of a circular letter written by Evgenios Voulgaris, a Greek hierarch who, from 1776–79, had been the archbishop of Kherson in Russia.

At that time there was a danger that the Orthodox Serbs would be forced to convert to the Greek Catholic church under Rome. Voulgaris had written that letter to persuade the Serbs of the evils of the Unia and the falsehood of the pope's claim to authority over the Byzantine church in Eastern Europe. The contents of the pamphlet in 1912 had little application to the Orthodox Serbs who at that time were not threatened by forced conversion to Rome, but the contents did contain some strong arguments suggesting that the Uniates should be reunited with the Orthodox church.[77]

The second pamphlet by Denasii, *The Athos Icon of Our Holy Virgin*, provided the strongest direct attack on the Greek Catholic church, the pope, and the Austrian government which, in the mind of the author, was a tool of the pope. In the pamphlet Denasii described in gruesome terms the "forced" conversion in the sixteenth and seventeenth centuries of the Galician and Subcarpathian Orthodox to the Unia with Rome. The resulting Greek Catholic church with its Greek rite was a fraud designed by the pope, according to Denasii, to deceive the peasants into thinking they were still Orthodox.[78]

Denasii's third pamphlet provided an account of the conversion of the Subcarpathian Uniate, Father Aleksei Kabaliuk, to Orthodoxy in a ceremony on Mt. Athos.[79] This pamphlet was written from the viewpoint of a Nickoli _____, a young man from Galicia who was searching for Orthodox truth on Mt. Athos. The monks there suggested that he as a Uniate could not participate in Orthodox blessings unless he renounced the Unia. This he did and served, according to the author, as an example for others to follow.

All of these pamphlets are interesting because they were not overtly pro-Russian propaganda but their contents were militantly Orthodox and anti-Catholic. Both the Austrian and Hungarian governments were aware that in the minds of the Rusyn people Orthodoxy and Russia were close to synonymous. Scattered throughout this devotional literature were prayers for the tsar and even for the Russian army.[80]

The reason the prayer books contained these references had been explained by Bishop Nicholas Ziorov of North America back in the 1890s when Russian immigrants were charged with being disloyal to America. The bishop argued that Russia was the defender of Orthodoxy around the world and the prayers for the tsar and the Russian army were prayers for the only real defenders Orthodoxy had in this world. They were not prayers for Russia as a nation in competition with other nations.

The enemies of the tsar, which the prayer book cursed, were not nations such as Austria or Germany, but rather they were the enemies of Orthodoxy.[81] With this argument Russian propagandists expected to neutralize the Austrian and Hungarian arguments that the Orthodox literature was treasonous. Legally there was religious freedom in both Austria and Hungary, but in practice Orthodoxy was persecuted in Hungary and only tolerated in Galicia.

The pamphlets of Denasii discussed above were more carefully written as propaganda than were the prayer books. Denasii's writing, while very bitter in its attack on the pope and the historical relationship between Rome and the Austrian Empire, circumspectly failed to endorse the Russian government as the liberator of the Austrian Slavs.

Both Austria and Hungary found it necessary to challenge this Orthodox propaganda in court, however. Some of the leading pro-Russian propagandists were arrested in both Lviv, Galicia and Marmaros, Hungary. Father Kabaliuk, the leading character in one of Denasii's pamphlets, was one of those arrested in Hungary. The Hungarian trial took place in Marmaros during February 1914. Denasii's pamphlets as well as others were introduced as evidence. Unfortunately, some of the other pamphlets were more direct in their praise of Russia as the protector of the Slavs. On 3 March 1914, Kabaliuk and thirty-two other Rusyns were sentenced to jail.[82]

The trial in Lviv started a week later and included much the same evidence and charges, but after deliberation, an all-Polish jury acquitted the Rusyns. The members of the jury were unable to satisfy themselves that the pamphlets were in fact treasonous. The defendants were able to satisfy the jury that their association with Russia was religious, not political.[83]

In the decade before the Great War, Russian involvement with the Rusyns in Galicia began as a continuation of the Pan-Slavic movement—different Slavic societies exchanging ideas on philosophical objectives. An analysis of these objectives demonstrated that the Slavophiles within the Russian Empire considered Slavic unity to be an expansion of Russian power, language, and influence, as well as Russian culture. The Slavs outside the Russian Empire had a far more egalitarian view of eventual Slavic unity as a federation of autonomous states and cultures.

As World War I grew near, the Russian government became interested in these Slavophile movements and through direct influence co-opted the leadership of these movements, transforming them into a propaganda arm of the Russian government. The leaders of most of the Slavic societies inside and outside of Russia, the leaders of the Russian Orthodox church, the military, the press, the nobility, and the government were all joined together as a united group in the Hunger Committee of the Galician-Russian Benevolent Society.

This committee led a subtle propaganda campaign, especially in Galicia. The committee's activities were so carefully protected, by the Orthodox church and the humanitarian objectives of feeding the hungry, that the Austrian government was unable to limit its activities.

In the case of Galicia, however, Russia's intentions need not be left to speculation since Russia occupied Rusyn Galicia during the first months of World War I. Count Iurii Bobrinskii, the brother of the president of the Galician-Russian Benevolent Society, was made governor general of Galicia and Archbishop Eulogii Georgievskii was appointed the bishop of Galicia.

In an interview with Count Bobrinskii, reported in *Tserkovnyi viestnik*, the governor general described Russian policy for Galicia. Galicia was divided along its ethnic lines with western Galicia being assigned to Polish territory. The future of western Galicia was as yet undecided, but the eastern part of Galicia was declared to be "an indivisible part of Russia."[84]

The Poles were allowed to maintain their Catholic churches, but the Uniate churches in eastern Galicia were "allowed" to "return to Orthodoxy." This return was to be based on a vote of the parish and Bobrinskii indicated that most parishes wished to unite with the Orthodox church.[85] On the matter of schools, Count Bobrinskii recognized only two options, Polish and Russian.[86] There was to be no toleration of Ukrainian. The fortunes of war, however, made this occupation only temporary and years of official and unofficial Russian organizing and planning came to naught as the German army aided the Austrian army in pushing Russia back out of Galicia.

3

The Influence of the Russian Orthodox Church on the Cultural Consciousness of the Rusyns in America

The Rusyns came to the United States from Galicia (and Bukovina) and northern Hungary. They spoke similar dialects of the same language, but in spite of repeated efforts they were never able to unite as a single ethnic group.

The majority of the Rusyn immigrants came to the United States as illiterate peasants and had not participated in the intellectual and cultural conflicts that were raging in the old country.[1] Thus it was in this country that most of them were first confronted with the opportunity to establish their own concept of nationality. It was in this country that Rusyn peasants from Galicia and Subcarpathia first lived together in the same community and found that they did not have as much in common as it at first seemed. It was in the United States that many of them first heard of the Ukrainian movement. And it was here that the Rusyns from Subcarpathia felt free to express national sentiments without the pressures of Magyarization. It was in the United States that most of the Rusyn immigrants were told for the first time by the Russian Orthodox mission that they were really Russians.

All these new cultural forces had a confusing effect on the Rusyn immigrants who would have been bewildered and lost in the new country even if they knew who they were. As millions of immigrants before them, the Rusyns wished to recreate something familiar that would remind them of the comforting security of the "old country." The church—their church—was the institution that could provide a social, cultural, and spiritual center for their lives much as it had in Europe.[2] It was because those peasant immigrants wished to reconstruct their heritage that they got caught up in the arguments over cultural identity that were being disputed among the intellectuals in their homelands.

The Rusyn immigrants were not initially aware of their different cultural perspectives when, on 12 February 1892, a group of Galician and Subcarpathian priests and laymen met together and organized the *Sojedinenije Greko Kaftolicheskich Russkich Bratsev* (Union of Greek Catholic Russian (Rusyn) Brotherhoods).[3] At that meeting the organizers also decided to publish a newspaper, *The Amerikansky Russky Viestnik*, but they did not have a formal name for the language they spoke. The paper was to be published in "Russian, but in Russian with a Slovakian dialect."[4]

The Greek Catholic Union, which became the English name of that organization, was organized by both Galicians and Subcarpathians. In later years the union was identified exclusively as a Subcarpathian Rusyn association but, as a Ukrainian writer observed, the Greek Catholic Union was founded by "Ugro Russians and a handful of Galician Russophiles." At least one brotherhood that formed that union was called Galician Ukrainian (in Shamokin, Pennsylvania) and one of the board members was Ukrainian.[5]

When several other Galician Rusyn brotherhoods joined the union, they recognized a serious difference between Subcarpathian and Galician interests. Perhaps they sensed "that it [Greek Catholic Union] was being controlled by magyarizing priests,"[6] but most likely there was a camaraderie among the majority Subcarpathians that did not include the Galicians. It is also likely that some Galicians were beginning to identify with the Ukrainian movement, and the Subcarpathians had no interest in that movement. At any rate, the Galicians formed a dissenting group and on 22 February 1894, they met in Shamokin, Pennsylvania, and formed an organization for Ukrainian immigrants called the Rus'kyj Narodnyj Soiuz (Rusyn National Union), now called the Ukrainian National Association.[7]

The organization the Galicians formed, the Rus'kyj Narodnyj Soiuz, should properly be referred to as the "Rusyn" National Association rather than "Ukrainian" at the time of its formation. (During World War I the organization formally changed the name to "Ukrainian.") The Rusyn National Association became the central organization for the Ukrainian movement but in 1894 it also included many Galicians who were later to identify themselves as Russians and who, as mentioned below, broke away from the Rusyn National Union and formed the Obshchestvo Russkikh' Bratstv' (Russian Brotherhood Organization).

In 1895, the third major society was formed reflecting another choice for the Rusyn community. That was the Russkago Pravoslavnago Obshchestva Vzaimopomoshchi (Russian Orthodox Mutual Aid Society), whose founding was inspired by Father Alexis Toth. Ironically, that society was also founded in the same church in Wilkes Barre, Pennsylvania, in which the Greek Catholic Union had been founded three years earlier.[8] This society was not only Orthodox but Russian. These three organizations still did not represent all the significant choices for the Rusyn immigrant.

In 1900, the Obshchestva Russkikh' Bratstv' (Russian Brotherhood Organization) was founded by a Subcarpathian Rusyn, Ivan Zincuk Smith. Smith joined with other Rusyns, who were dissatisfied with the Ukrainization of the Rusyn National Union, to form the new organization. The Russian Brotherhood Organization membership consisted primarily of Galician Rusyns who were anti-Ukrainian. For the most part the organization took a pro-Russian stance and published in literary Russian with occasional Rusyn dialect.[9] This organization immediately found it had a serious problem. Its membership included both Orthodox and Greek Catholics, so in 1902 it banished priests from membership to limit the arguments that divided its members.[10]

The division in the Russian Brotherhood Organization suggested the divisive nature of the cultural and religious conflict within the Rusyn community, especially between 1900 and the First World War. Each society viciously criticized the other societies and Orthodox and Greek Catholics viciously criticized each other.

The *Kalendar*, an annual publication of the Russian Brotherhood Organization (RBO), published a poem written by Mikhail P. Baland who was the general controller for the RBO. The poem was entitled "Do russkikh' molodtsev" (To Russian Youth):

You are the sons of Holy Rus'! . . .
May the land of your mother remain dear to your heart . . .
The Poles and Jews would subvert you with the idea of "Ukraine"
An ideal land in which there are no Polish landlords and no Jews.
That is double talk
No such land exists.
Study the history and writings of Rus'.
And thereby strengthen your resistance to the Ukrainians.
And you will grow to be proud sons of Mother Rus'.[11]

The Russian Brotherhood Organization was obviously anti-Ukrainian. But the "Rus' " in the poem does not necessarily mean "Russia." It is a more abstract term that was also used by the Ukrainian Galicians to refer to their homeland. Other poems in that *Kalendar* such as "Nasha Rus' " (Our Rus')[12] suggest an emotional and romantic attachment to the physical properties of the Rusyn homeland, the valleys, the mountains, streams, forests, etc. But beyond that very basic identity with the valley or village of one's birth, the members of the Russian Brotherhood Organization were also pro-Russian.

The Greek Catholic Union was also opposed to the Ukrainian movement. An article in its almanac, *Mesiatsoslov' Soedineniia* (Almanac of the Union) for 1912 attacked those who opposed the objectives of the Greek Catholic Union. The author noted that the Galician Greek Catholics would like to merge all the Rusyns in this country into a single movement. "But the Galician Rusyns are agitating for Ukraine and are filled with the Ukrainian spirit. . . . But the Greek Catholic Union is fairly immune to that movement because its character is entirely Ugro-Russian."[13]

The Greek Catholic Union leaders were fairly confident that the Subcarpathian Rusyns would not be influenced by the Ukrainian movement. "But," the writer continued, "the Union receives its greatest threat from one of its own Ugro-Russian priests, Alexis Toth, the leader of the Russian schism. This Russian schism is very dangerous and the Union and its paper have taken a strong stand against it."[14] The ultimate objective of the leaders of the Greek Catholic Union was to "organize the Rusyns to promote Rusyn religious-nationality uniting in America all Rusyns from Subcarpathia."[15]

The Greek Catholic Union by 1912 was trying to identify its members with an idea of nationality that included the Greek Catholic rite as an identifying factor. This concept was opposed by the Ukrainian movement, which was primarily a secular movement. The concept was also opposed by the Russian Orthodox church, which supported an opposing religious-ethnic identity. The Galician Rusyns began to identify with the Ukrainian movement, especially after 1895, when several young priests came to the United States "imbued with the spirit of Ukrainian national revival."[16] From then on, the Rusyn National Union and its newspaper, *Svoboda*, became the voice of the Ukrainian movement.

Name calling among these various factions often became intense. In its impact on the Rusyns in the United States, the name calling perhaps began with the Russian religious press. In 1896 an article in *Tserkovnyi viestnik* (published in St. Petersburg, Russia) charged that "the arm of Jesuit strength is working in America."[17] The article identified the Ukrainian-Uniate activity in America as inspired by the Jesuits. It further charged that the newspaper *Svoboda* was the "tool of the Sons of Loyola" and that the main purpose of the movement (Ukrainian) was to stop the growth of Orthodoxy among the Galicians and Subcarpathians in America.

In 1899, *Svoboda* carried an article entitled "The Sting of the Russian Knout." The article accused the Russian Tsar Nicholas II of identifying himself as the "Tsar of all Russians." By implication that included the Russians who lived in America "where McKinley is our President." "His [the tsar's] arm in America is the Orthodox Church and the *American Orthodox Messenger* is his voice."[18]

Criticism that the tsar was the political leader of the Russians in America had evidently been raised before. The Russian Orthodox bishop (in America), Nicholas Ziorov, had addressed that issue in a sermon in 1892, subsequently published in a bilingual article in the *Russian Orthodox American Messenger* in 1896.[19] Nicholas observed that, in fact, the Russian Orthodox church did respect the tsar and his family by declaring their birthdays to be "high feast days." He was aware that some may object by suggesting that such celebrations are right in Russia but not in America where "the majority of the congregations are not Russian subjects at all."

Nicholas responded that it was wrong to renounce native customs; if these customs were renounced, the immigrant may soon renounce Orthodoxy itself. Such celebrations, however, are not political and have nothing to do with Caesaropapism. The Russian emperors have two separate roles: They are political leaders of the Russian people in Russia. But they are also "zealous guardians and defenders of Orthodoxy all over the world." That does not mean that they are heads of the Russian Orthodox church—they are not, the Holy Synod is—but they should properly be honored and prayed for by Orthodox around the world because they are the foremost defenders of Orthodoxy.[20] Nicholas's explanation appeared strained and was probably a variation of the classical Russian argument refuting the charge of Caesaropapism and did not entirely respond to the new situation in America.

From the preceding survey it is obvious that the Rusyn immigrants were exposed to an unprecedented amount of cultural conflict. In reality they were a people who did not have a developed sense of nationality. It was this very unsettled cultural and religious environment that the Russian government and the Holy Synod decided to exploit in the name of mother Russia and Holy Orthodoxy.

The Russian Orthodox church was first established on the North American continent in 1794 when eight monks from the Vallaam Monastery in Finland landed on Kodiak Island off the coast of Alaska.[21] These monks arrived there six years after the merchant-trader, Gregory Shelekhov, first petitioned the Holy Synod to send missionaries to this newest territory under Russian exploration.[22]

The reasons for this delay are not entirely clear. Part of the delay was due to bureaucratic lag, but the basic reason for the six-year delay was more likely the Russian church's concept of its mission. Apparently, the Russian Orthodox church did not feel that it had a mission outside its borders and the territory of Alaska had not been formally integrated as a Russian province. Another problem arose from the concept that baptism into the Russian Orthodox church conferred the rights of Russian citizenship upon the convert. This concept had to change in 1867 when Alaska was sold to the United States and many thousand Russian Orthodox citizens of Russia became American citizens.[23]

In the treaty that transferred the land to the United States, the rights of the Orthodox church and its members were to be protected.[24] The Russian citizens were given the option of returning to Russia or being granted American citizenship. In determining who should be granted citizenship in the United States, baptism was again a significant factor, since the treaty offered citizenship to all the "civilized" people.[23]

In spite of the transfer of the territory from Russia to the United States, the Russian Orthodox church remained. The church continued to be served, staffed, and subsidized by the Russian mother church as a missionary institution.[26] Thus, after 1867, the Russian Orthodox church became a mission church to non-Russians outside its borders. It was this missionary institution that spread its influence down the Pacific coast to California establishing churches among the Russian immigrants there.

Finally, in 1891–93 the church made a radical departure from the tradition of its North American mission. It launched an effort to convert Greek Catholic Rusyns to Orthodoxy. In effect, the decision to reach the Rusyns in America was an extension of the policy being implemented in Eastern Europe. The policy was different, however, because Russia had no claim, real or imagined, to "Rusyn territory" in North America.

The Orthodox church established its hierarchical organization in America with the appointment of its first bishop, Joasaph, one of Alaska's original eight monks, in 1799. Unfortunately, Bishop Joasaph was killed in a shipwreck on his way back to the Alaska Islands. The Holy Synod failed to appoint a second bishop until 1840 when Alaska's greatest missionary, John Veniaminov, was consecrated as Bishop Innokentii. Bishop Innokentii served as the bishop in Alaska for a dozen years before being recalled to Russia. After some years, he was appointed the metropolitan of Moscow, the highest-ranking prelate in the Russian Orthodox church at that time.[27]

In the early 1860s there were no Orthodox churches in the United States. By the end of the decade there were only three and they had established themselves independently of each other. In San Francisco there was a Russian Orthodox congregation. In New Orleans, there was a Greek Orthodox congregation and in New York, there was a second Russian Orthodox church founded by members of the Russian consulate there.[28]

The center of Orthodoxy in 1870 on the North American continent was clearly Alaska where 25,000 of the 33,000 native population (Eskimo, Aleuts, and Indians) were at least nominally Orthodox.[29] In 1872 Bishop John Mitropolsky transferred the bishop's cathedral from Sitka to the church in San Francisco. This move was approved by the Holy Synod a few years later during the administration of John's successor, Bishop Nestor (1879–82).[30]

It is difficult to determine why the bishop's cathedral was moved from Sitka to San Francisco and why the Holy Synod approved that move. It does not seem likely, as has been suggested, that the episcopal see was transferred to San Francisco in recognition of "the potentialities of Orthodoxy in the United States."[31]

In 1872 there was very little potential for Russian orthodoxy in the United States. The Rusyn-Greek Catholic immigration had scarcely begun and the Russian Orthodox church had never proselytized other Christians. The best judgment is that the bishop wished to move his see outside the territory of the American military dictatorship ruling Alaska under General Davis.[32] Bishop John then established his cathedral near the Russian consulate in San Francisco.

It was in San Francisco, in December 1890, that two representatives from St. Mary's Greek Catholic Church in Minneapolis
contacted the Russian Orthodox bishop. These representatives
arranged for the Greek Catholic congregation of St. Mary's to
convert to Orthodoxy. Thus a movement began that was to result
in the conversion of over one-third of the Rusyn immigrants.

The events leading to the conversion of this Greek Catholic
congregation were outlined many times by the chief participant,
Father Alexis Toth.[33] Construction was started on St. Mary's in
Minneapolis in 1887. The church was built and owned by the
members of the congregation since they had no priest and were
not at that time associated with any diocese. When the church
was finished, the congregation wrote to the bishop of their home
diocese, Prešov, in northern Hungary (now in eastern Czechoslovakia). After some delay, Bishop John Valyi sent Father Toth
who held a doctoral degree in canon law from the Greek Catholic
seminary in Uzhhorod.[34] Father Toth held his first service at St.
Mary's on Thanksgiving Day, 1889.

On 19 December 1889, Father Toth visited Archbishop John
Ireland of St. Paul to present his credentials and receive authorization to administer the sacraments at St. Mary's.

Bishop Ireland had some knowledge of Greek rite Catholics in
Eastern Europe, but he along with most of the bishops in America were convinced that the Latin rite alone should represent the
Catholic church in the United States.[35] When Bishop Ireland
read from the credentials that Toth was a "Greek Catholic," he
became upset. Father Toth remembered the dialogue that followed in Latin as follows:
The bishop asked:

—Do you have a wife?
—No! I answered.
—But you did have?
—I am a widower . . .
When he heard my answer, he threw the papers on the table and
loudly exclaimed:
—I already sent a protest to Rome, not to send me such priests . . .
—What kind do you mean?
—Such as you . . .
—But I am a Catholic priest of Greek Rite! I am a Uniat! I was
 ordained by a lawful Catholic Bishop . . .
—I do not consider you or that Bishop a Catholic; Furthermore, I
 have no need for Greek-Catholic priests, it is sufficient that in

Minneapolis there is a Polish priest, he can also be priest for the Greek Catholics . . .

—But he is of the Latin Rite; our people cannot understand him; they will not go to him for service—it is for that reason that they built themselves a separate church . . .

—I gave them no permission to build, and give you no jurisdiction to act in any capacity here.[36]

When that conversation was terminated, Father Toth reported back to his congregation at St. Mary's. There is no accurate account of what happened during the next year, but it was not until the following December that the congregation wrote to the Russian consul general in San Francisco, asking for the name and address of the Russian Orthodox bishop. Perhaps Father Toth suggested the "Orthodox" alternative or perhaps the congregation convinced Father Toth that conversion to Orthodoxy would be better than submitting to the Latin rite with a Polish priest.[37] After some correspondence, Bishop Vladimir Sokolovsky visited St. Mary's congregation and accepted the congregation and its priest into the Orthodox church on 25 March 1891.[38]

Neither the Russian government nor the Russian Orthodox church initiated the conversion of the first Uniate congregation to Russian Orthodoxy. The conversion of that congregation was sparked by the refusal of Bishop Ireland to accept a Greek Catholic priest into his diocese. Even after Bishop Vladimir accepted St. Mary's congregation into Orthodoxy, it took the Holy Synod until July 1892 to sanction officially the new congregation.[39] But that one instance convinced the Russian church that the Rusyn immigrants in the United States should be converted to Orthodoxy to complement the Orthodox work among the Rusyns in Eastern Europe.

The second Greek Catholic congregation to convert to Orthodoxy was located in the center of the Rusyn immigrant population, Wilkes Barre, Pennsylvania. The church was also called St. Mary's Greek Catholic Church. The congregation had organized themselves and built their own church. They were unable to get a Greek Catholic priest on their terms. So they called Father Toth of Minneapolis to advise them on joining the Russian Orthodox church.[40]

Father Toth arrived in Wilkes Barre on 3 December 1892. After only a few days' discussion, the congregation accepted Toth's terms for joining the Orthodox church. One of those terms included deeding the church property to the Orthodox bishop who was the newly appointed Bishop Nicholas Ziorov of San Francisco. On 13 December Bishop Nicholas informed the congregation that he had accepted them into the Orthodox church. This acceptance must have been granted by return mail with no hesitation on the part of the bishop.

Just six months later on 9 July 1892, Bishop Nicholas planned an elaborate dedication of the church.[41] Bishop Nicholas presided over the dedication, but he was assisted by two chaplains from two Imperial Russian warships then docked in New York. The choral responses to the liturgy were sung by the crewmen of the warships under the direction of Lieutenant Nazimov.[42]

The Russian campaign to convert the Rusyns to Orthodoxy was not conducted by the Russian church alone. From the beginning, the Russian government actively participated in that movement.

Father Toth, the priest who encouraged the conversions, was given the rank of *Protoierei*, archpriest, and notice of his work was brought to the attention of the Government Council (Gosudarstvennoe Sovet). The council pledged that it would pay an annual stipend from the imperial treasury of 2,200 rubles for the maintenance of the parish in Minneapolis.[43] This stipend from the imperial treasury indicates a direct governmental support for the conversion activities among the Uniates in the United States. Such direct support was never again noted in the Synod's annual reports.

In 1895, the Holy Synod decided to move the cathedral for the North American eparchy from San Francisco to New York.[44] In 1895 it was not yet true that the eastern United States had a greater Orthodox population than Alaska, but with a continued emphasis on the conversion of the Uniates, the population center soon shifted to the east.

In 1897, the Holy Synod made a more extensive report on the activities of the North American eparchy. The report indicated that in the last five years the composition of the Aleutian eparchy had completely changed. The majority of the people in the eparchy were no longer the natives of the Aleutians and Alaska, but an entirely new people who "are of Russian spiritual heritage." The report noted that the transition, for the most part, had been very satisfactory.[45]

In 1899, the Holy Synod contributed $600 toward the publication of *Svit*, the Russian Orthodox Mutual Aid Society's publication, because "it was of significant interest to the Little Russian Uniates who converted to Orthodoxy."[46] In 1899 Tsar Nicholas was given a report of the mission work among the Uniates in America and he responded, "I personally donate 5,000 rubles to this great Christian work."[47] In October 1899, the Holy Synod voted to contribute 43,988 rubles to the work of the American Churches and missions.[48] This contribution was a significant increase over the previous commitments and was to increase considerably in the following years.

In the following year, 1900, Tsar Nicholas was informed of the building of the cathedral in New York. He again responded with exactly the same words he had used the previous year, "I personally donate 5,000 rubles to this great Christian work." The tsar's 5,000-ruble donation was part of a fund-rising campaign in Russia that raised 60,000 rubles toward the construction of St. Nicholas Cathedral.[49]

In 1900, the tsar also placed the North American mission under the "protection" of the Orthodox Missionary Society.[50] This "protection" did not mean that the North American mission was removed from the direct jurisdiction of the Holy Synod and placed under the Missionary Society. It meant that the Orthodox Missionary Society was authorized to extend its interests to include the North American mission. In fact, the Orthodox Missionary Society never did play a significant role in America nor did it place a high priority on its American responsibility.

The Orthodox Missionary Society was founded by Metropolitan Innokentii of Moscow in 1869. Bishop Innokentii was known as Father John before he was admitted to the Holy Orders. He performed as an outstanding missionary while he served the Aleuts and Indians in Alaska.[51] The Missionary Society was established to work within Russian Imperial territory. The tsar, however, had specifically placed both Japan and North America within the society's scope of responsibility.[52]

The society's basic method of operation was to build schools among the non-Christian people in order to provide the young with the basic education required by the state and, at the same time, teach them the fundamentals of Orthodox Christianity.[53] This method of missionary work could also be adapted to Japan and Alaska since neither place had a compulsory education system. However, that system was not readily adaptable in eastern United States among the Rusyns. The Rusyns had willingly accepted the public education system and the English language teaching requirements for private schools were too stringent for the missionary society.

These circumstances probably explain why the Orthodox Missionary Society, while accepting some responsibility for the North American mission, limited its activities to Alaska by aiding in the support of the forty missionary schools there.[54] But even in Alaska, their commitment was never very great. For example, in 1903 the society's budget for missionary endeavors, primarily education, was 350,415 rubles. Of that, 170,528 rubles were spent in Siberia; 110,480 rubles were spent in European Russia; 25,128 rubles were spent in Japan and only 5,000 rubles spent on the North American mission and all of that was spent in Alaska.[55] Thus the Orthodox Missionary Society played no acknowledged role in the conversion of the Rusyns to Orthodoxy.

While the Orthodox Missionary Society did not contribute to the Synod's missionary work among the Rusyns in the United States, the tsar continued to support that work from his personal treasury. In 1901, he donated a second 5,000 rubles to the cathedral in New York, 5,000 rubles for an Orthodox church in Chicago, and 2,000 rubles for an Orthodox church in Pittsburgh.[56] In 1908 he donated 5,000 rubles for the establishment of a Russian Immigrant Home in New York.[57]

The most active secular institution in the conversion campaign was the Russian Orthodox Mutual Aid Society. A representative of official Russia also participated in the founding of the society in Wilkes Barre in 1895. The society's founders and organizers were Archbishop Nicholas, Father Toth, and the Russian consul general in New York, A. E. Olarovsky. The consul general also served as the first president of the society from 1895–97.[58]

This society was founded with three basic objectives. It was to be a mutual aid society to look after the physical needs of its members. It charged dues and from its treasury it paid out set amounts if a member should be injured. It paid for funeral expenses if the member should die. The society also aided orphans and widows of deceased members.

The society required that all of its members be members of a Russian Orthodox church. Among its objectives were the propagation of the Orthodox faith among non-Orthodox Russians (Rusyns) and the nurturing of its members in the Orthodox faith.

Finally, the society wished to promote cultural awareness. In its founding statement the organization declared that the society was to be Russian and that there was one undivided Russian people.[59] This last statement was significant since nearly all the society's members were from the Austrian Empire. The society also was the only American society authorized by the Holy Synod of the Russian church. This authorization was announced in Ukaz no. 4703, 27 September 1895.[60]

The church leaders were generally members of the society, and the society's printing press did most of the printing for the Russian Orthodox church. The newspaper *Svit* and its annual *Kalendar* served as the official publications of the Orthodox church. *Svit*, more than any other newspaper in this country, expressed the official position of the Russian Orthodox church and very often expressed the viewpoint of the Russian government.[61] The local chapters of the Russian Orthodox Mutual Aid Society were generally associated with the local Russian Orthodox congregation in that area. Local chapters of the society, together with the local congregation, generally sponsored reading rooms in the local church. These reading rooms were vehicles for the propagation of Russian language, literature, and politics.[62]

While the conversion of the Rusyns to Orthodoxy fit into the greater plans of the Russian government for annexing the Rusyn territory in Eastern Europe, the church leaders did have a genuine religious concern for the people. The Rusyn immigrants were responsive to the Russian overtures for entirely different reasons. The Rusyn immigrants in the United States were divided by many competing cultural and social forces, and, in their search for stability in a strange land, the Russian church offered a stable cultural tradition in which they could comfortably participate.

It is difficult to find a persuasive reason why the Orthodox bishops moved the bishop's cathedra from Sitka to San Francisco in the 1870s, but the reason for the second move from San Francisco to New York in 1903 was clear.[63] The Russian Orthodox church wished to move its administrative center closer to the new Rusyn population. It had not overlooked the fact that the new immigrants, who might be attracted to the church, were almost entirely Greek Catholic Rusyns from the Austrian Empire.

Bishop Nicholas, who led the Orthodox mission in the United States from 1891 to 1898, "was instrumental in accepting into the Orthodox church over 25 new parishes from the Unia."[64] From then on it is fair to say that the primary orientation of the Russian Orthodox church in America was directed toward converting the Uniate Rusyns to Orthodoxy.

During his tenure in the United States, Bishop Nicholas established many of the foundations for an effective missionary movement, which Archbishop Tikhon Belavin was to develop further. Nicholas established a missionary school in Minneapolis, aided Father Toth in founding the Russian Orthodox Mutual Aid Society, printed the first Orthodox periodical in America, the *Russian American Orthodox Messenger*, and encouraged the Mutual Aid Society to publish its weekly newspaper, *Svit*.[65]

During Archbishop Tikhon's administration from 1898 to 1907, the Archbishop received over thirty-five parishes from the Greek Catholic church.[66] Tikhon immediately set about building the bishop's cathedral in New York. The money for this purpose was largely raised in Russia with Tsar Nicholas II supporting the drive by donating 10,000 rubles "towards this important Christian work."[67]

The Russian Orthodox mission in the United States also received about $70,000 annually from the Holy Synod and the Russian Missionary Society of Moscow.[68] The receipt of these funds was severely criticized by the opponents of the Orthodox church in the United States, generally Greek Catholic or Ukrainian spokesmen. The Greek Catholics correctly felt that the Orthodox church was in competition with the Greek Catholic church and the success of Orthodoxy would be at the expense of the Greek Catholic church. The Ukrainians felt that the Orthodox church offered more than just a religious orientation; to become Orthodox was to become Russian. Thus Ukrainian historians have observed that "The objectives were political as well as proselytizing,"[69] and the Russians were "trying on American soil to convert them to Russian Orthodox religion and make Russians of them."[70]

The conversion of Greek Catholic Rusyns to Orthodoxy is controversial but, nevertheless, interesting. What provided the Russian cultural offensive with its élan? How was the Russian mission able to convert over one-third of the Rusyn immigrants to Orthodoxy and to convince them that they were Russians?

First of all, the $70,000 to $75,000 annual subsidy was helpful, especially when the infusion was directed to the top of the hierarchy. The local congregations would protect their own interests first and send limited amounts of money to the bishop. The Orthodox mission would have had little money for missionary purposes if it had not been for this infusion from Russia.

Iuliian Bachyns'kyi, a Ukrainian writer, observed in 1914 that, while a number of Greek Catholic priests flirted with Orthodoxy, all the Greek Catholic priests returned to Greek Catholicism except Father Toth, who remained in the Russian mission. Thus, the Orthodox churches were staffed by priests from Russia.[71] From this observation it is also clear that the Rusyn priests did not lead the people into Orthodoxy.

The Russian Orthodox *Kalendar* for 1950 gave the following statistics: From 1891 to 1898, twenty-five new parishes were admitted to Orthodoxy from the Unia. From 1898 to 1907 there were an additional thirty-five; and from 1907 to 1914, under Archbishop Platon, over one hundred new parishes were organized, most of them former Greek Catholic parishes.[72] These figures seem high since the 1901 Orthodox *Kalendar* and the Ukrainian *Svoboda* seemed to agree that by 1901 only thirteen congregations had converted to Orthodoxy.[73]

However many parishes there were, they needed to be staffed with priests. Since very few Greek Catholic priests converted to Orthodoxy, the Russian Mother church had to provide priests for all of those congregations.

During Bishop Nicholas's administration in the 1890s the Holy Synod sent at least eleven priests to the United States. These priests included some who were to become leaders in the Orthodox church in America for many years. They were representative of the best educated and talented young priests that Russia could offer. They held degrees from the best theological academies in Russia. Three of them were graduates of St. Petersburg Theological Academy.[74]

During that same period, Bishop Nicholas encouraged the new Rusyn congregations to send their brightest young men to the Minneapolis missionary school. This school offered preparatory training for a theological academy. Bishop Nicholas picked the five most promising graduates of that school and sent them to theological academies in Russia for their training. Peter Dzubay, Alexander Veniaminov, and Paul Chuberov were sent to the St. Petersburg Theological Academy, Peter Kohanik to the Seminary of Tavrida in Simferopol, and Nicholas Metropolskii to the Don Theological Seminary.[75]

These individuals returned as priests along with a continuing supply of new Russian priests during the administration of Archbishop Tikhon. Thus, clerical leadership of the Rusyn congregations was Russian. The Russian priests established church schools within their parishes to teach Russian language and literature as well as Orthodox doctrine.

Archbishop Tikhon recognized that the church in America should not be entirely dependent on Russia for its priests and the training of priests. Early in his administration Tikhon changed the mission school in Minneapolis into a theological seminary. Again, Tikhon was able to staff the school with well-trained theologians from Russia. They included Leonid Turkevich who had received his Doctor of Theology degree from Kiev Theological Academy. He was appointed dean of the Minneapolis seminary and years later became the metropolitan of the Russian Orthodox church in America.[76]

Another teacher was Michael Ilyinskii who received his Doctor of Theology degree from St. Petersburg Theological Academy. In 1946 he associated with the Moscow patriarchate and was appointed patriarchal exarch of North and South America with the rank of metropolitan.[77] Another of the teachers was V. M. Bensin. Dr. Bensin received his Doctor of Theology degree from the Moscow Theological Academy. In later years he taught at St. Vladimir's Seminary in New York.[78] There were several other very talented teachers at the seminary. It was obvious that the Holy Synod wished to make the American mission a showcase of Orthodoxy with a Russian orientation.

The Russian priests and church leaders took full advantage of the talents of the young Rusyns who attended the missionary school and the seminary. Peter Kohanik was a good example of that generation. He was born in Becherov, in the Prešov area, in 1880. His parents emigrated to the United States when he was a child. They were members of a congregation that joined the Russian Orthodox church. Peter was talented so his father sent him to the Russian missionary school in Minneapolis from which he graduated in 1898. From there he was sent to the Simferopol Theological Seminary in Russia. When he graduated in 1902, he returned to the United States and aided Father Toth in organizing Orthodox churches among the Rusyn immigrants.[79]

From that time on Peter Kohanik was an active publicist for Orthodoxy and Russia. For years he was the editor of *Svit;* he wrote several histories of the Russian Orthodox Mutual Aid Society and he regularly contributed anti-Uniate articles to the Russian Orthodox *Kalendars.* During World War I he vigorously defended the Russian government in a pamphlet entitled *The Austro-German Hypocrisy and the Russian Orthodox Greek Catholic Church.* This pamphlet and many other small articles were written in English in an attempt to appeal to a wider readership than those who could read Russian. His *Nachalo istorii amerikanskoi rusi* (Early History of the American Rus') has been republished.[80]

This work and most of his others were published in literary Russian and indicate how thoroughly Peter Kohanik had accepted Russian culture as his own. He argued repeatedly that there was one Russian people and that the Rusyns were members of that family. He took pleasure in pointing out that the Ukrainian National Association was founded as the "Russian National Union."[81]

For the most part the Rusyn youths who were educated in Russia or in the Russian Orthodox Theological Seminary in this country adopted the same perception of their cultural identity as did Peter Kohanik.

There was one other group of leaders among the Rusyn immigrants, especially from Galicia, who aided in the development of Russian culture among the Rusyns but who did not necessarily identify with the Orthodox church. These were the founders of the Russian Brotherhood Organization. This society broke away from the Rusyn (Ukrainian) National Association in July 1990, because the latter had developed a Ukrainian orientation.[82] While not all members identified with the Orthodox church, Mr. Lutsik, the second editor of the Russian Brotherhood's newspaper, *Pravda*, did convert to Orthodoxy in 1908. He used his leadership position to further the causes of Orthodoxy and Russian culture.

A Hungarian priest in the Greek Catholic church, Rev. John Korotnoki, reported to the Austro-Hungarian consul general in Philadelphia that Lutsik had converted to Orthodoxy and was now planning a visit to Galicia and Hungary. There he would tell the people that "while a Greek Catholic, he was living in darkness, but since becoming an Orthodox he was beginning to see the light." Korotnoki asked the consul general to take the necessary steps to prevent that visit.[83] While the missionary effort of the Russian Orthodox church was led primarily by Russian priests and Russian-trained priests, the church leadership also sought to convert Rusyn leaders to Orthodoxy and to encourage those converts to influence their followers to become Orthodox also.

The Russian Orthodox Mutual Aid Society served as a major institution in attracting the Greek Catholic immigrants into the Orthodox church. As a transmitter of Russian culture the society was an interesting and effective institution even though it never had as many as 10,000 members at any one time. The society's membership grew steadily from 696 in 1896 to 7,862 in 1911. From then on the membership leveled off but increased in the war years of 1917 and 1918 to over 9,000. After those two years, its membership dropped back to 7,500 in 1919 and generally has declined ever since.[84]

Every president of the society from 1895 until 1910 was an immigrant from the Russian Empire. The first was the Russian consul general and the rest were priests sent by the Holy Synod as missionaries to serve the American mission.[85]

Peter Kohanik, the second Rusyn to be elected president of the society, was first elected in 1912 and served as president for several terms. In 1915 while he was still president, he wrote the twenty-year anniversary history of the organization. In that history he wrote:

> The society is dedicated to fight for Orthodoxy wherever it is threatened. We must help not only in a moral but also in a material way. Therefore we have already sent $600 to Austria with the aim of liberating Orthodoxy from tyranny.[86]

This quotation suggests how closely the leadership of the Mutual Aid Society identified with the aims and objectives of the Orthodox church. It indicates that even the Rusyn leaders of the society identified the concepts of "Russian" and "Orthodox" as indivisible as far as the objectives of the society were concerned. It also indicates how closely the Russian mission in America was associated with the Russian cultural objectives in Eastern Europe.

The close association between the Mutual Aid Society and the Russian Orthodox church had also been emphasized in 1907 when Archbishop Tikhon suggested at the seventh convention of the society that the church press, which published *The Russian-American Orthodox Messenger*, be merged with the society's press, which published *Svit*. This merger was accomplished and the single enterprise, *Svit*, published both papers.[87]

Benedict Turkevich, a Russian who was born and educated in Russia, was the president of the society from 1907 to 1910. He also wrote a history of the Mutual Aid Society. In that history he supported a very singular view of nationality and of the role of the Mutual Aid Society. He wrote:

> In the last decades of the 19th century, thousands of ethnic Russians of the Uniate faith came from Hungary and Galicia to North America. At the same time the majority of immigrants from Austria were Uniates who very quickly showed an interest in Orthodoxy. Our American Orthodox mission met them with open arms and great sympathy. Gently, through reasoning and without fanatical haranguing, they invited their brother Uniates to join the Mutual Aid Society.
>
> The Society then had a dual aim—to provide material help to the new Russian immigrants and to help them get established in the Orthodox Church. . . .
>
> Members of the Society must be completely Orthodox brothers without other nationality [bez' drugikh narodnostei].[88]

It was typical of the Russian missionary priest to view the Rusyn immigrants as "ethnic Russians." It is also interesting to notice how the terms *Orthodox* and *Russian* could be interchanged. To the secular mind *Orthodox* suggests a religious grouping while *Russian* suggests a nationality or ethnic grouping. Yet in the last paragraph quoted above, Benedict Turkevich used Orthodox as a nationality grouping when he said "members of the Society must be completely Orthodox without other nationality."

Benedict Turkevich also demonstrated another "Russian" attitude that probably explains why so few Great Russians came to America (hundreds of thousands of Russian Jews came) while so many Slavs from the Austrian Empire came. In 1911 when Turkevich was the editor of *Svit*, the Mutual Aid Society's newspaper, an article appeared entitled "The Question about Farms." This article was only initialed by "B. T.," but it is very likely that the author was Benedict Turkevich.[98]

The author complained about the mass exodus of "Russians" from Austria and Romania. He was not complaining because they were leaving the Austrian Empire: he was complaining because they emigrated to America. He felt that "Russians" should migrate to Russia. According to the author, the "Russians" that migrate to America get jobs in the large cities and in the coal and iron mines. While there "they are irresistibly drawn to the soil and many of them buy farms in the states."

The author noted that many of these immigrants "are successful and happy—praise God, of course." But he deplored the loss to Russia that these people should leave their homeland. "How can she [Russia] correct the imbalance when the happiness of those who leave Russia is not adequate compensation for the loss their absence causes those who remain."

The author recommended as a solution that those who wished to emigrate should immigrate to the Caucasus:

> There one can buy land in the Caucasus all the same without the burden of leaving Russia to become Americans. . . . And it goes without saying that you will still be Russians in the land of your birth with the Russian culture and church. The Russian people have suffered much in their hour, and as far as that goes, America aided Japan in her war against Russia.[90]

The author also deplored the exodus of Poles and Jews from Russia. On this point he criticized the Russian officials for being so shortsighted that they actually encouraged the Poles and Jews to leave so the Russians could get the land they left behind.

The article is indeed very curious, especially in its muted but real anti-American flavor. The author's main argument is that the emigration hurts mother Russia. This argument may be true when applied to the Poles and Jews who left Russia, but they were, as was suggested, pushed out by officials who were anxious to see them go. The "Russians" or Rusyns from the Austrian Empire had never been a part of the modern Russian state and it is difficult to see how their leaving Austrian territory could hurt Russia. Finally, the number of ethnic Russians who left Russia was in fact very small. Emily Green Balch analyzed the immigration statistics for 1905, one of the few years for which the country of origin was properly noted. She said that less than two hundred ethnic Russians came from Russia proper in that year.[91]

The author of "The Question about Farms" was more emotional than analytical. But perhaps the opinion he wished to express was that the Rusyns from Galicia and northern Hungary were Russians; their leaving for America to become Americans made them permanently lost to Russia—and ultimately Russian culture. If they had emigrated to the newly settled lands in the Caucasus and Siberia, they could have been joined to the Russian land and made a positive contribution to themselves and to Russia.

That interpretation suggested that the author had not constructively adapted to the role of an Orthodox missionary in the United States. His view on that subject may have been shared by other early missionaries from Russia. But his was not the prevailing view among the leaders of the Rusyn community nor was it the prevailing view among some other leaders of the Orthodox church. The Russian Orthodox mission occasionally did serve a constructive role in helping the immigrants adapt to their American environment. But on the whole the Rusyn laymen led the Orthodox church in adapting to life in America.

Theological and theoretical arguments seldom lead to mass conversions; while the Russians did use these arguments, the conversion or "the return to Orthodoxy" of the Rusyns was based on a far more practical missionary endeavor.

A letter in Svit in 1911 indicated how the Orthodox church could gain influence in a community. The writer wrote about his community, Rockdale, Illinois, which consisted of about fifteen hundred to two thousand residents; "all are immigrants and all come from the Austrian Empire—Galicians, Hungarians, and

Croatians—and from Russia—Lithuanians, Poles, and Russians."[92]

In this community there was evidently significant interaction among people with similar languages. So it was significant when, according to the letter writer, two brothers, Nikolai and Peter Mikitchuk, were instrumental in opening a branch of the Russian Orthodox Mutual Aid Society there. Such a local brotherhood could be small, perhaps with only four or five members and could precede the organization of an Orthodox church. The writer indicated that the purpose of the brotherhood, of course, was mutual aid, but also its "main purpose was to unite people with the national faith of the land of their birth (Orthodoxy)."

If the Mutual Aid Society brotherhood was successful, an Orthodox parish would be organized and perhaps a chital'nia (reading room) would be established. The reading room was generally located in the church building and was the primary vehicle for cultural education in a Russian Orthodox parish. The reading room was often funded by donations from the local brotherhood of the Mutual Aid Society and books, no doubt, were often furnished by the Russian mission.

Many "correspondents" for Svit described the activities of their local reading rooms. Father M. Fekula, from Coldale, Pennsylvania, wrote that during the evenings:

> People meet in the reading room and read newspapers and books from both America and the old country. The leaders discuss the burning issues of the day, especially the plight of all the Russian people in Galicia who are persecuted by the Poles and their followers—the Ukrainians who are the lackeys of the Poles.[93]

Father Leonid Turkevich of Minneapolis had a more complete description of the reading room there. He wrote in Svit that during 1910 the reading room held sixty-six meetings. Of these thirty-five were classes in reading, twenty-seven were of the lecture type, and two were semiannual business meetings. The reading classes were divided into four courses. The "fourth-year" class—the highest—had sixteen students, which included two women. Three members of that class were "exceptional." The second- and third-year classes each had about thirty-four members. In addition to the organized classes, the reading room served as a library for those who wished to stop in and read books and newspapers. Father Turkevich listed the more significant newspapers the reading room received. They were:

Novoe vremia—from Russia.
Russkoe slovo—from Galicia.
Nedelia—from Budapest.
Pravda—from Olyphant, Pennsylvania.
Svit—from New York.
Amerikansky Russky Viestnik—the publication of the Greek
  Catholic Union.[84]

In 1972, Peter Yurkovskii wrote in *Svit* about his memories of
the Russian reading room in Mayfield, Pennsylvania, many years
earlier. He wrote that the parish school was founded in 1900 and
taught Russian history:

> All of these activities were in the Galician-Russian dialect, very close
> to the literary Russian. . . . In literature biographies of the presidents
> of the United States were read and studied. Children read the chil-
> dren's poems of Pushkin, Lermonotov, and other famous poets of
> Russia. Krylov's fables were a delight. Most of the literature was in
> literary Russian. . . . *Svoboda* Ukrainian-American newspaper was
> read until it became an organ of the treacherous followers of
> Mazeppa, rather than the true followers of Saint Vladimir.[95]

These reports indicate that the reading rooms were both pro-
Russian and anti-Ukrainian and did much to impress the Orthodox Rusyn that he was a Russian.

In 1905, Archbishop Tikhon made his report on church reform. In that report he described the parish organization of the
Orthodox church in the United States. Each parish had an annual
meeting that reflected the shared control of church policy. The
auxiliary activities were also quite different from those of the
church in Russia.

> Most congregations maintain a place for a school and a reading room.
> In every parish there is a brotherhood. The brotherhoods invariably
> bear a church character: They choose a saint as their patron. From
> their funds they support the church, pastor, schools and the church
> building. Besides that they pursue spiritual objectives. They help
> their members: They serve the sick, maimed, unemployed, and they
> settle disputes between members. In general, the brotherhoods here
> are very popular and associated with the "Orthodox Mutual Aid
> Society."[96]

Tikhon's description of parish activity suggested that there was
a significant amount of lay control and leadership of parish

activities. To the potential convert, the Orthodox parish looked very inviting as a center of activity within the newly established Rusyn community.

Public concerts also advertised the Russian Orthodox message. A *Svit* correspondent wrote about a "spiritual-secular concert" in Scranton with Russian spiritual and secular songs." The Greek Catholics evidently tried to prevent a good turnout since the correspondent wrote "they tried to frighten our weak-minded blood brothers, the Uniates, telling them not to go to the 'Muscovite' concert." But "both Americans and Uniates, to say nothing about our own people" came to the concert.[97]

The Russian mission also had another voice in the Rusyn community that could be quite effective among immigrants who could read and were starved for reading material in an understandable Slavic language. The newspaper *Svit* published by the Mutual Aid Society served an invaluable function as described by "letters to the Editor." In such a letter, in 1911, a writer from Fayette, North Dakota, wrote that until a friend gave him a copy of *Svit*, he had only the socialist paper *Russkii golos* (Russian Voice). Since he began reading *Svit*, he no longer needed the socialist paper. Before reading *Svit* he did not even know there was an Orthodox church in America so he was "assigned to a Polish Catholic Church 20 miles away" (no doubt he was a Uniate). He closed his letter with the wish: "Now if only someone could send us an Orthodox pastor."[98]

In 1912 a new Russian language newspaper appeared. It was called *Russkii emigrant'*; it was published independently of *Svit* and the Russian Orthodox Mutual Aid Society, but it was printed on the same press as *Svit*. Its articles and editorial viewpoint were the same as that of *Svit*, and the two papers carried advertising encouraging subscriptions to the other paper. Apparently, the Russian mission wished to extend the reach of the newspaper medium by publishing a secular newspaper not associated with a specific organization.

The letter responses to *Russkii emigrant'* were similar to those in *Svit* with the writers indicating that they no longer had to read the socialist newspapers, *Russkii golos* and *Novii mir* (New World).[99] However, the letters in *Novii mir* indicated that the newspapers were battlegrounds between the Orthodox and the secular Russian community. A letter in *Novii mir* under the heading "Why I don't read *Russkii emigrant'*" said:

I read *Novii mir* because it is the newspaper of the worker but *Russkii* emigrant' is the servant of barons and counts and titled people and I can never be sure of the truth of that which is printed in *Russkii emigrant'*.[100]

The newspapers *Svit* and *Russkii emigrant'* were widely read even by the non-Orthodox Rusyns, because those who could read Russian would read anything published in that language to keep them in touch with others in the immigrant community and in the homeland.

The attraction of socialism and workers' unions to the Rusyn immigrant concerned the Russian mission very much. In February 1911, Bishop Alexander Nemolovsky published an open letter in *Svit* attacking Ivan Okuntsov who was then the editor of *Russkii golos*. The letter opened with the phrase "Renegade Return" and degenerated into a series of epithets attacking Okuntsov for his anti-Orthodox views. "Only in free America is such vocal murder, lies, violence, and injustice allowed." Alexander's letter had no specific criticisms but his attack on the competing organizer was unrelenting. He closed with the phrase, "Your name will forever be Judas the Betrayer."[101]

Alexander was so bitter in his attacks because Okuntsov was a competing organizer attempting to unite the Russian-Rusyn community in America. Okuntsov's efforts were directed toward establishing a single "Russian" immigrant organization with a secular perspective rather than an Orthodox perspective. In 1914, an article in the socialist newspaper, *Novii mir*, which was sympathetic to Okuntsov, endorsed Okuntsov's work and deplored the opposition he had encountered from the Orthodox church. The writer indicated that Okuntsov had been trying to establish a single organization that would unite the whole Russian colony in America. He ran into stiff opposition from the "divisive factions in the community that speak through the hooligan-papist-Tsarist newspaper, the *Russkii emigrant'*." The writer concluded that "perhaps it is better for the Russian community that these factions are not included in a general organization."[102]

There was a real conflict between the workers' organizations and the Russian mission. The mission was antisocialist while most of the worker organizations, often local unions, were dominated by socialists. But even in the less abstract realm of day-to-day work, the Russian mission and *Svit* served as a voice for the employers.

In many of the areas where the Rusyns worked, 1912 was a year of arrests and strikes. Yet *Svit* regularly carried accounts of good working conditions and high-paying jobs. The 25 January 1912 issue contained an editorial that began: "The General Manager of Davis Colliery, J. F. Healy, wrote us." The editorial described how a zealous worker could earn seventy-five dollars a month, pay only seven dollars a month rent on a six-room stucco home in an area that had not had a fatal accident in three years.[103]

In June 1912, a letter by Father Zaichenko of Lyndora, Pennsylvania, told how "the workers, grow fat because there is a need for more workers."[104] During the same month there was a report published from Pittsburgh, indicating how many jobs were available there with good pay.[105]

In June 1912, that attitude may have changed. An issue of *Svit* carried the headlines of a "Strike in Perth Amboy." The supporting article seemed to be sympathetic to the workers especially when it was noted that many of those injured in the clash with police had "Russian" names.[106] That same issue also carried a letter signed "Striker" from Hastings-on-Hudson, New York. "Striker" reported a strike of over two thousand workers. Most of the workers there were "Russians from Austria-Hungary." They struck the National Conduit Cable Company because they were getting only $1.50 a day for a ten-hour day and these small wages were docked because the workers could not understand English.[107]

The editor of *Svit* seemed to be sensitive to such news as Russians being beaten by police and workers being docked for not understanding the foreman's English, because later issues avoided accounts of working conditions from the employers' point of view.

In October 1912, *Russkii emigrant'* sorrowfully carried a report of a vote held by one of the workers' organizations in New York. The Russians at that meeting subcaucused to determine which calendar they should follow in dating their Russian language newspaper. The vote was overwhelmingly to follow the "American method." The reporter indicated "that this was a severe blow for orthodoxy since the Russian holidays must be celebrated by the old calendar."[108]

Such a vote was insignificant in itself but the church leaders made a big issue of it. The issue indicated the division that existed between the Russian-born priests and the Rusyn peasant immigrants. Most of the Russian priests and church leaders did not intend to stay in the United States. They were just missionaries. Leonid Turkevich, a typical missionary, came to the United

States at the turn of the century and was appointed dean of the seminary in Minneapolis where he also served as the pastor of Saint Mary's congregation. He was a respected leader in the Russian Orthodox church and in the 1950s was elected metropolitan of the North American metropolia. But he did not become an American citizen until the 1920s because he had intended to return to Russia; it was only the Russian Revolution that led him to realize that he would never return.[109]

In spite of this typical attitude toward Americanization among the Russian leadership, Bishop Nicholas, who supervised the initial missionary effort to win the Rusyns to Orthodoxy, published the *Russian-American Orthodox Messenger* in both English and Russian. He established the missionary school in Minneapolis where English was taught and many classes were also taught in English. He also commissioned Isabella Hapgood to translate the Russian liturgy into English.[110] These steps may seem minor, but they were taken at the very beginning of the mission's activity among the Rusyns and did establish an atmosphere encouraging the Rusyns to adapt to life in America.

Archbishop Tikhon continued the example set by Nicholas. When Ms. Hapgood's translation was finished, he authorized it to be used in worship services. But more significantly, he started the American mission on the way to autonomy in America. He foresaw a time when the Russian Orthodox mission in America would be independent of its mother church and mother country.

As discussed earlier in this chapter, Tikhon established the Orthodox Theological Seminary in Minneapolis so that the new generation of priests could be selected from among the immigrants in America. Because he was the archbishop here, Tikhon had a chance to describe his plans for the American mission in some detail. In 1905, the Russian church was discussing reforms and soliciting the recommendations of all its bishops. In his response to the reform committee Tikhon made a number of suggestions for the North American mission.[111]

He suggested that the North American mission should be given a fair degree of autonomy "because they [the Orthodox in America] are composed not only of a different national heritage [narodnosti] but also of different Orthodox churches which, while united in faith, have had a different canonical formation."[112] The Russian Orthodox church had canonical authority over all Orthodox in America, however Tikhon suggested, the hierarchy should not be excusively Russian. Under a Russian archbishop, each major Orthodox nationality should have its own bishop. For that reason he had appointed Raphail Hewa-weeney, a Syrian, as bishop of Brooklyn. Tikhon further recommended that a Serbian bishop be appointed for Chicago with responsibility for the Serbian Orthodox in America. There should also be a Greek Orthodox bishop but he did not know which city should be the center for that see.[113]

Tikhon's recommendation for national bishops was reasonable. According to the *Kalendar* for 1910, published by *Svit*, there were only 33,334 Russians and Rusyns and 55,483 other Orthodox in North America in 1910.[114] Tikhon wrote:

> We do not in truth wish to infringe on the national character of the local church, but just the opposite. We are endeavoring to preserve this heritage for them; let them if at all possible be placed directly subordinate to a leader of their own nationality.[115]

Tikhon apparently had a balanced view of the role of the Orthodox mission in the United States. He genuinely wished to establish an Orthodox church there. For that objective to be successful, the non-Russian nationalities would have to be encouraged to maintain their own traditions. He was not an advocate of Russianizing the Orthodox church in America. However, he apparently considered the Rusyns to be Russians.

Archbishop Tikhon developed the institutional framework that allowed the Russian mission to become an American Orthodox church. But it was left to Father Toth to show the Rusyn immigrants how they should personally adjust to their new land.

Father Toth had a remarkable background. He had the credentials to be identified as a Hungarian, Slovak, Rusyn, or Russian. *Toth* is the Magyar word meaning "Slovak," yet he identified himself with the Rusyns until he converted to Orthodoxy. From then on he generally identified himself as a Russian but never severed his Slovak connections. In 1899 he wrote an article entitled, "How We Should Live in America." It appeared in *Národný Kalendár*, the annual publication of the National Slovak Society.[116] In this article, Toth explained that it was possible to be a good American citizen and yet maintain one's cultural and ethnic identity.

Toth explained that there were "nativist" elements in the United States that wanted to restrict immigration to exclude the Slovaks and the Slavs whom they called "hunkies." Toth suggested that the Slovaks should shun behavior that would provide justification for the "nativist" arguments. His advice included,

"Keep your house clean!" "Don't send your children to the saloons with lunch pails for beer or spirits." "When you go out, dress cleanly." "Don't shout, howl and fight; if you do, you end up in jail and have to pay legal damages." "Don't shout, sing and insult God on the streets! You're lucky the policeman doesn't understand your blasphemy because there are strict laws against that."

These were a few of the "don'ts" Toth wished to impress on the immigrants. He also emphasized that they should learn of their heritage, which was in this case, Slovak.

> At home, always converse in Slovak with them [children] for the hope of each nation lies in its youth and if they forget their mother tongue, they will forget their nationality and it will die out. . . . Love and treasure your nationality! If you are a Slav, you are a brother to all Slavs. . . . Do not trust those Hungarian scoundrels who wish to divide you by country. . . .
> Learn the English language, and if you can, attend night school. . . .
> Take out American citizenship if you wish to live here! . . .
> If you behave yourself as I have suggested, my dear Slavic brothers, then never will anyone hold anything against you and no one will downgrade you but rather will regard you as a proper, upright, honest citizen and friend and in this way you will acquire glory for yourself and for us all.[117]

That was the advice of the Russian mission's most effective missionary among the Rusyn Greek Catholics. Father Toth intended to remain in the United States and wished to teach his immigrant fellow citizens how to live in America.

Many of the enemies of the Russian mission charged that "through the Orthodox Russian Church here a powerful effort is being made to prevent immigrant Slavs from becoming Americanized and to bring them into allegiance to the Czar."[118] The work of the Russian mission in the United States could be interpreted in that way. Many of the Russian missionary priests may have been more interested in introducing the Rusyns to Russian culture than to American culture. But the bishops generally recognized the need to encourage American citizenship and to develop the Orthodox church in America as something more than an "arm of the Tsar." The Rusyns themselves also found it necessary to respond to their new environment in a positive rather than a negative way. Perhaps Father Toth's formula was a workable one! Perhaps an immigrant could be faithful to his cultural heritage and yet be a good American citizen.

If the Russian mission could be faulted, it was not because it prevented the Americanization of its members. Perhaps it could be faulted for substituting a Russian tradition for the Rusyns' heritage, but in doing so, the mission had provided a voluntary option for Byzantine rite Rusyn immigrants who had been deprived of their normal ethnic and religious options by Latin bishops, Hungarian nationalists, and as will be discussed later, a Greek Catholic bishop who was ordered by the pope to enforce practices contrary to their Eastern European traditions.

The Russian mission was successful to a very high degree in converting the Rusyn immigrants to Orthodoxy and grafting a form of the Russian cultural heritage onto the Rusyn identity. Many third-generation descendants of Rusyn immigrants know only that they are Russian. Yet they are curious when they discover that their grandparents' home village is in eastern Czechoslovakia.

4

Hungarian Cultural and Nationalistic Activity within the Greek Catholic Church in America, 1900–1907

In 1901 the prime minister of Hungary[1] was informed that some Rusyn emigrants to America were returning to Hungary and were convincing their covillagers to convert to Orthodoxy. This conversion was a serious threat to the government, since the government associated Orthodoxy with Russian imperialism. In the fall of 1901, the minister of religion ordered an investigation to determine the extent to which Russian Orthodox teaching was being accepted by the Greek Catholic priests and people.[2]

The investigators determined that a number of Rusyns had emigrated from Becherov (north of Prešov now in eastern Slovakia) to Minneapolis, Minnesota, where they had been converted to Orthodoxy by Father Toth. Some of them had returned to Becherov and were successful in convincing the villagers that they should convert to Orthodoxy. The investigators further determined that it was only the lack of a church building that prevented a large number of villagers, including priests, from converting to Orthodoxy. Furthermore, a Russian organization in America had promised to raise money for that purpose.[3] There was considerable concern over the Becherov incident. Some officials feared that it was the beginning of a trend.

The district attorney, Janos Paksy, charged that more than one-third of the population was leaving the Greek Catholic church and demanding a Russian Orthodox pastor. This, he argued, was encouraged by the rumor that after the death of Emperor Franz Joseph, the Rusyn territory in northern Hungary would be ceded to Russia and therefore it would be to the Rusyns' advantage to convert to Russian Orthodoxy.[4]

The district attorney also suggested the prosecution of several priests—Andras Zbihlej, Vasil Zbihlej, and Laszlo Tutko—on the charge that they were spreading anti-Catholic propaganda.[5] On

19 March 1902, those three were indicted on the propaganda charge.[6]

The outcome of the Becherov investigation was to have a significant impact on the Rusyn immigrants in the United States. In the final report to the prime minister it was recommended, as Bishop Valyi had suggested earlier, that the Greek Catholic church should send representatives to America to stop the influence of the antipatriotic priests on the Greek Catholic Rusyns in the United States.[7]

Since Hungary had diplomatic channels to the Vatican, an initial request was immediately authorized and two representatives were sent. Andrew Hodobay, a canon of the Prešov diocese, was sent as an apostolic visitor and John Korotnoki was sent as a priest to Allegheny, Pennsylvania.[8]

The writer of the report also suggested that it would be necessary to send to America a vicar general (bishop) who would have more authority than an apostolic visitor. This vicar general should not only be a prelate, "but a political agent as well." In order to realize this objective, "the Vatican should be given more evidence about the Russophile movement among the immigrants who have returned to northern Hungary from America and Russophile-Orthodox influence there."[9]

This plan was implemented by the prime minister. For the next five years, the Hungarian government tried to persuade the Vatican to allow the Hungarian government to nominate a bishop for the Greek Catholics in America. In the report to the minister outlined above, the representatives of the church were also to be active "political agents."[10]

According to Hungarian government statistics published in Budapest in 1902, there were 262,815 Rusyns in the United States. Rev. Hodobay, the apostolic visitor, estimated that 70 percent or 190,933 of them came from Hungary while the remaining 30 percent or 81,829 came from Galicia. These people were originally Greek Catholics served by eighty-five mission parishes, but the report noted that many had converted to Orthodoxy. As many as 1,500 in Bridgeport alone had converted to Russian Orthodoxy.[11]

The Hungarian government misunderstood the problem, however. The government strategists felt that the lay people were, more or less, docile followers of the priests and it was the priests who were leading them astray. Early in 1902 the Hungarian government issued several policy orders designed to limit the priests who went from Hungary to America. The priests were to be faithful Magyars who would support Magyarization of the Slovaks and Rusyns in America rather than work against it.

This policy was explicitly outlined in Ministerial communication no. 393 from the Hungarian minister of religion, Komlossy, dated 4 February 1902, which was sent to the Catholic hierarchs in America.[12] This communication argued that the Hungarian government must look after the several thousand Hungarian citizens who had emigrated to the United States, since these people, especially the Ruthenians (Rusyns) were subject to Pan-Slav temptations. Furthermore, many of these immigrants had converted to Russian Orthodoxy and returned to Hungary.

The communication noted that the Hungarian government was taking several steps to protect its interests in the United States. The government would prevent "hostile" priests from emigrating to America. It would specially select and send only "well-disposed" priests. Therefore, American bishops should accept only priests with proper credentials. These steps were very necessary, according to Komlossy, because among the forty-two Slovak Roman Catholic congregations in America only seven of them were led by "patriotic priests."[13]

Somehow that communication got leaked to some Slovak priests. They translated it into English and wrote an interpretation of it that suggested the Hungarian government was interfering in the internal affairs of American citizens. In December 1902, they published the letter and interpretation and sent a copy to the State Department.[14]

In their letter of interpretation, the Slovak priests noted that Mr. Komlossy's adjectives describing the priests, "well-meaning," "well-disposed," "eligible," and "patriotic," were not spiritual attributes but rather political attributes. The type of priests being discussed were "priests who are in accord with the existing policy of the Hungarian Government which contemplates the forcible Magyarization of the people coming from Hungary." Such a policy, they argued, interfered with Americanization.[15]

That communication and the Slovak priests' interpretation were published as a pamphlet under the title, *Hungary Exposed: Secret State Document Reveals the Plotting of that Government in the United States*. On 26 July 1903, the *Washington Post* picked up the story and ran a summary of the Slovak account.

The following day the *New York Times* interviewed Joseph Horvath, the editor of the Hungarian-American newspaper, *Szabadsag*.[16] Joseph Horvath demonstrated a total inability to understand the American point of view. He did not argue the factual contents of the Slovaks' charges; he just restated the Hungarian view that such a policy was necessary. He argued that in the old country the Slovaks and Rusyns "pretend to be loyal to Hungary" but when they come to America, "they generally parade with the Russian colors at their head." He further noted that back in Hungary the traditional language for the Greek Catholic rite was "Russian," but since some Hungarians belong to that rite, the Hungarian government now requires that the services be in the Hungarian language. He finally suggested that the purpose of the edict was to "avoid sowing the seed of disloyalty among those who go back to Hungary."[17] His response merely indicated to the American newspaper readers that minorities in Hungary did not enjoy American-style freedoms.

This policy of pressuring the minority nationalities resident in Hungary to become Hungarians or Magyars has been called "Magyarization." Perhaps the "idea" had more merit than its implementation. The Magyars did not exclude people on account of "race" as did the German nationalists. Anyone, in some cases, even a Jew, could become a Magyar. The people in Hungary were expected to adopt the Magyar language. The people in Hungary could worship according to their own faith: They could be Lutheran, Calvinist, Greek Catholic, or Roman Catholic. Thus Hungary under the Magyars was more accepting of religious diversity than many other countries in Europe. It is true that they were very suspicious of Orthodoxy because they identified it as "Russian"—but then the Russians also identified Orthodoxy with Russia. In essence Magyarization was intended to be a unifying force in Hungary. Somehow, however, when unification is forced, that unifying force becomes destructive, and so it was with Magyarization among the minorities in Hungary.

When Rev. Andrew Hodobay, the Hungarian apostolic visitor, came to the United States in 1902, he understood that the Greek Catholic Union with its newspaper *Amerikansky Russky Viestnik* was the central cultural institution for the Subcarpathian Rusyns in America. One of Rev. Hodobay's first acts was to attempt to remove Paul Zhatkovich as editor of *Amerikansky Russky Viestnik*. He was unable to have Zhatkovich removed at the union's biannual meeting in 1902, so he sought to have him extradited from the United States to Hungary. The Hungarian prime minister had discovered that Paul Zhatkovich had been arrested and indicted for misappropriating funds in Hungary in 1892, but had avoided jail by escaping to the United States.[18]

The extradition proceeding failed, according to Hungarian authorities, because the summons could not be served on Zhatkovich since his "address was unknown."[19] It is more likely that the American authorities considered Zhatkovich a political refugee rather than a criminal escapee.

When it became obvious that the Greek Catholic Union with its newspaper *Amerikansky Russky Viestnik* was led by anti-Magyar laymen, the Hungarian government considered establishing its own newspaper for the immigrants in America. Rev. Hodobay was to supervise the editing of this paper and it was to be printed in the native languages of the immigrants from Hungary; it was to be printed in Magyar, Slovak, and Rusyn.[20] However, after an extended discussion between Hungarian representatives in the United States and Hungary, that plan was postponed indefinitely because of the high cost and technical problems involved in publishing a multilingual newspaper that would most likely have a limited readership.[21]

The two newspaper incidents mentioned above were only minor attempts to influence the Rusyn immigrants in America. The major strategy, developed with the full participation of the Hungarian prime minister and the Imperial Foreign Ministry, was to get a Hungarian Greek Catholic selected by the pope as the bishop of the Greek Catholics in America. This imperative was spelled out in detail in the report to the prime minister in 1902 regarding the Becherov incident.[22]

At that time the pope had already authorized Bishop Valyi of Prešov to select an apostolic visitor to investigate the need for a Greek Catholic bishop in the United States and to act as a mediator between the Greek Catholic churches and the Latin bishops. Beyond that, however, the apostolic visitor, Hodobay, had no real power.

The Hungarian government was confident that, with Hodobay in America and the Hungarian government's representatives in good standing in the Vatican, it would not be difficult to persuade the pope to appoint a Hungarian Greek Catholic bishop who would be a patriotic "political agent" for the Hungarian government as well.[23] In spite of this support from Europe, Andrew Hodobay was not to have an easy task because the Greek Catholic church in America was divided by so many incompatible interests that it would have been virtually impossible to create a united organization.

Hodobay's assignment was twofold. As a representative of the Holy See, he was to investigate the total situation of the Greek Catholics in America, make annual reports to the Vatican, and regular reports to the apostolic delegate in Washington. These reports were to give the Vatican the information necessary to determine if the Holy See should establish a diocese for the Greek Catholic rite in America.

From the papal perspective, those responsibilities would seem to be Hodobay's primary function, but the Hungarian government and Bishop Valyi of Prešov had already determined that such a diocese was necessary. Hodobay was also fully committed to the concept of a Greek Catholic bishop in America.[24] As a representative of the pope, Hodobay also served as a mediator between the Greek Catholic priests and the Latin bishops. This was an important but thankless function. The bishops were not inclined to accept his advice because he was not of their rite. The priests and the people were suspicious of him because he was pro-Magyar.

Hodobay's second role was that of a political agent for the Hungarian government. This role was generally a secretive one and is confirmed only from his correspondence with the Hungarian prime minister.[25] The leaders of the Greek Catholic Union, however, suspected his connection with the government and often aired their suspicions in *Amerikansky Russky Viestnik*.[26]

As a political agent, Hodobay was to slant his reports to the pope in such a way as to influence the pope to appoint a bishop that would be acceptable to the Hungarian government.[27] He was also to recruit and organize the Greek Catholic priests who were loyal to Hungary and encourage them to sway their congregations to become loyal Magyars, something they had failed to become back in Hungary.[28] This task was to be accomplished by identifying the unpatriotic priests in the United States, having them recalled, and sending in their places only "good and faithful priests" selected by a council of Hungarian bishops.[29]

The objective of the Hungarian plan was to win the allegiance of the Rusyn immigrants in the United States through the Greek Catholic church. In order to suppress "Pan-Slavic" and Rusyn nationalistic ideas among the immigrants, it would be necessary to develop a strong Greek Catholic church organization supported by the Hungarian government.[30] Thus the heart of Hodobay's political mission was to develop a strong Greek Catholic church organization staffed with Magyar priests dependent on the Hungarian government. It is easy to see how his responsibilities to the Holy See were closely connected to his political activities. Again it should be emphasized that this plan assumed that it was the pastors, not the lay people, who were the source of "unpatriotic activities."

The first step in the Magyarization of the Greek Catholic priests in America was implemented in Hungary. In a letter to the apostolic delegate in Washington, Hodobay informed the delegate that a selection committee had been established in Hungary. This committee was composed of seven bishops, two were Greek Catholic and five were Latin bishops. The committee was to select and prepare priests from Hungary to fill vacancies in the Greek Catholic parishes in America.[31] No doubt the committee placed significant emphasis on the patriotism of the candidate priests.

The committee's selection procedures were probably quite successful. In the early period of migration, the priests more or less selected themselves and presented an undisciplined and independent if not anti-Magyar group. But by 1918 a significant majority of the priests from Subcarpathia voted that in the postwar settlement, Subcarpathia should be joined to the new Hungary. This opinion was, however, reversed by a congress of lay people from Subcarpathia.[32] The vote by the priests indicated that the composition of that body had changed considerably in the years between 1902 and 1918. An alternative explanation may suggest that the priests never were as "unpatriotic" as the Hungarian government suspected.

Rev. Hodobay, as an agent of the Hungarian government, was responsible for evaluating the priests in the United States and the activities of their organizations. In a letter to the Hungarian prime minister in February 1906, Hodobay wrote that the most active and most patriotic Hungarian Greek Catholic priest of the past year was Julas Orosz of Cleveland.[33] In June of that year, Hodobay wrote another letter to the Hungarian minister encouraging him to send more "patriotic priests," and also informing him that there was an "anti-patriotic" campaign led by Rev. Julius Medvecky of McKeesport; "He tries to separate people from the Hungarian Government."[34]

Hodobay and his associate, Rev. John Korotnoki of Allegheny, also reported on the political impact of the biannual meetings of the Greek Catholic Union. Korotnoki and Hodobay tried to influence the decisions of these meetings but failed in every instance. About the 1904 convention of the Greek Catholic Union, Rev. Korotnoki wrote to the Hungarian prime minister that the Slovak P. V. Rovnianek and his "panslav" supporters had a decisive

influence on the convention. The three most "detrimental" results were that President Michael Yuhasz, Sr., of the "panslav"
group was reelected, a resolution was passed requiring that all
high officers be American citizens, and the convention incorporated "the Panslav spirit and rules in the form of an oath."[35]

Korotnoki's 1906 report on the Greek Catholic Union Convention focused on the establishment of a "National Fund" that
was to support Rusyn ideas in opposition to Magyar ideas among
both the Rusyn immigrants in the United States and the Rusyn
population in Hungary.[36]

Finally in 1908, the Austro-Hungarian consul in Philadelphia
wrote the Hungarian prime minister that priests who represent
the interests of the Hungarian government are fully excluded
from the Greek Catholic Union. He reported that the leadership
of that organization was taken over by Paul Zhatkovich who was
elected editor of the newspaper, Amerikansky Russky Viestnik,
for life.[37] Thus Hodobay's efforts to build a pro-Magyar base
within the community's most important association failed completely.

Hodobay was also charged with the political responsibility of
organizing as many Magyar-speaking congregations as possible
within the Greek Catholic church. This was not an easy task
since most of the Magyar-speaking Greek Catholics had settled in
areas where the Rusyn-speaking immigrants dominated the congregations. A separate Magyar-speaking parish was not always
feasible. Ultimately Rev. Hodobay was able to establish five
Magyar-speaking parishes in: Homestead, Cleveland, Passaic,
Bridgeport, and South Lorain.[38] It took a considerable amount of
effort on the part of Hodobay to establish some of these churches
since the bishops were not always convinced that two or more
Greek Catholic churches in a single area were necessary.

Hodobay's efforts to establish a Magyar-speaking parish in
Homestead are very instructive since they illustrate his method
in overcoming the bishop's strong opposition. In July 1905, Hodobay wrote a letter to the Bishop John Canevin of Pittsburgh
indicating that the Magyar-speaking people in the Homestead-
Duquesne-McKeesport area had requested that he help them
organize a Magyar-speaking Greek Catholic church in that area.
In his letter Hodobay asked the bishop for permission to investigate the request and promised that "if, after investigating it, it
appears that their numbers are too few to support a priest I will
do all I can to discourage them."[39]

Bishop Canevin responded, giving Hodobay permission to attend but reminding Hodobay that there were already two Greek Catholic churches in the area. Therefore, the people "should be dissuaded from the notion of organizing a third" because "the support of the two would be lessened and an additional burden would be imposed on the poor people without necessity."[40]

At the meeting Hodobay passed on the bishop's admonition, but he determined that there were 176 families and 280 single persons who were Magyar-speaking Greek Catholics.[41] Hodobay wrote to the bishop that:

> In spite of my repeated admonitions the Hungarian people voted to organize a church. . . . Owing to these facts, I who am the representative of the Holy See for the Greek Catholic Church, beseech your Grace to give in any case your approval for the forming of this congregation which will be on your Name, otherwise I will have to submit the matter to the Propaganda [Sacred Congregation for the Propagation of the Faith].[42]

Hodobay's letter was reenforced by a petition from the newly elected officers of the Magyar parish. The petition explained, in poor English, the need for a separate Magyar parish:

> The race-prejudice of the Slavs whose prejudices are consistently nursed by their so-called Pan-Slavistic leaders, who bear against us, Magyars, the most Godless hatred, who sow discontent into our hearts of the Slavs, even against our co-religionists of the hated Magyar race, makes it impossible for us to worship in the same church.[43]

In spite of the passionate plea by the Magyar parishioners, Bishop Canevin rejected the request for a separate Magyar-speaking church. Hodobay was furious and threatened to appeal the decision all the way to Rome if the bishop did not reverse himself.[44] When the bishop did not change his mind, Hodobay appealed to the apostolic delegate in Washington. But the apostolic delegate recommended that Hodobay not press the appeal because that appeal might jeopardize the Sacred Congregation's consideration of a bishop for the United States.[45]

Upon receiving a negative response from the apostolic delegate, Hodobay wrote to the Hungarian prime minister and asked him to pursue the matter as he saw fit.[46] Hodobay's letter to the prime minister was dated 12 September 1905, and the archives do not indicate how the prime minister pursued the matter. But on 20 April 1906, Bishop Canevin wrote Hodobay announcing that he had appointed a committee to inquire into the need for a church for the Magyar-speaking people in the Homestead area.[47]

Evidently the Hungarian prime minister had gone over the head of the apostolic delegate in Washington. A Hungarian representative at the Vatican had evidently persuaded the Sacred Congregation to authorize the founding of a Magyar parish in Homestead. At any rate, a Magyar parish was founded there.

Not all bishops, however, were uncooperative in allowing Magyar parishes to be formed even when there were existing Rusyn Greek Catholic parishes. Hodobay began efforts to establish the Magyar church in South Lorain, Ohio, about the same time as he first attempted to found the Homestead parish. On 20 July 1905, Hodobay wrote to the Imperial and Royal Vice Consulate of Austria-Hungary in Cleveland.

> In response to your letter of the 17th the matter of the Hungarian Greek Catholic Church for South Lorain is now under the decision of the Right Reverend Bishop of Cleveland.
>
> I have informed the Bishop that it is impossible for the people of Hungarian tongue to worship with the people of Ruthenian tongue.
>
> I feel the Bishop will comply with my request.[48]

Also in July 1905, Hodobay set about to organize a Magyar Greek Catholic church in Passaic, New Jersey. Bishop John O'Connor of Newark cooperated fully even though there were already two Greek Catholic churches in the area and the bishop feared that the two Rusyn churches would have serious financial problems if some of their members left to form a third church.[49]

In December 1906, Hodobay wrote to the Hungarian prime minister indicating his progress in preliminary efforts to establish the Magyar parish in Passaic. At that time he asked for final authorization to proceed with the organization, and requested the prime minister to send a Magyar priest to serve the parish.[50]

While Hodobay established the Magyar church in Bridgeport, Connecticut, the Austro-Hungarian consul general in New York worked directly to establish a Magyar-language elementary school in Bridgeport. The school was to be administered by the Hungarian parish there. For that purpose, the consulate retained a lawyer, Arpad A. Kremer, to investigate the legal problems in establishing such a school. Kremer reported that there would be no problem in establishing such a school even with a teacher "imported from Hungary." But the students would not be allowed to enter high school unless they could pass a comprehensive test and demonstrate a "fair knowledge of English."[51]

The establishment of these Hungarian parishes and the school in Bridgeport indicated a retrenchment of the Magyarization effort among the Greek Catholic people. Hodobay and the consulates did not begin these efforts, however, until July 1905, after Hodobay had been here three years. Apparently, their first effort had been directed toward influencing the Rusyn people directly, especially members of the Greek Catholic Union. But when these efforts failed, they developed the strategy of founding Magyar-speaking congregations wherever they could find a concentration of Magyar sympathizers. Their next effort was to focus on the selection of a Hungarian bishop.

The apostolic delegate in Washington had realized the need for a Greek Catholic bishop in America as early as 1893, but there is no evidence the Hungarian government urged that the rite be transplanted to the new country at that time.[52] By 1902, when the Russian Orthodox church was unquestionably successful in converting Greek Catholics to Orthodoxy and to Russian culture, the Hungarian government recognized the need to develop the Greek Catholic church as a vehicle for Magyar interests. The value of the Greek Catholic church as a weapon against Russian Orthodoxy was the lesson the Hungarian government learned from the Becherov investigation discussed earlier in this chapter.

In October 1904, Rev. Hodobay sent the first report to the Hungarian prime minister that urgently requested the appointment of a Greek Catholic bishop for the United States. The report told about the "dangerous plan of Alexis Holoshnay and his group." Apparently "Holoshnay and his group" wanted the Greek Catholic priests and the people to nominate the bishop so they could be assured the bishop would be independent of the Hungarian Committee of Bishops and of the Hungarian government. Hodobay continued the report asking that the prime minister convince Rome that the Hungarian government should nominate the bishop and thus insure that the selection be made "in the patriotic interests of the Hungarian Government."[53]

Hodobay tried to recruit the Latin bishops to support his position requesting the pope to appoint a Greek Catholic bishop to the United States. Since most of the Latin bishops were opposed to the establishment of a second rite in America, that was not an easy task. He managed to use their letters to him to indirectly support his requests. For example, when the archbishop of Philadelphia and the bishop of Pittsburgh complained to him about the insubordination of the Greek Catholic priests, Hodobay forwarded their letters to the Hungarian prime minister with the suggestion that the letters be used to persuade the pope that only a Greek Catholic bishop could control the priests.[54]

Bishop Eugene Garvey of Altoona did, however, agree that the appointment of a Greek Catholic bishop would be the only solution to his problems with the Greek Catholics. Bishop Garvey wrote to Hodobay indicating that he had informed the apostolic delegate of his position and "the sooner a Bishop was appointed for them, all the better."[55] Hodobay also forwarded Bishop Garvey's letter to Hungary for inclusion in the battery of letters in the Hungarian government's arsenal for its campaign to convince the pope of the need for a second rite in America.[56]

From the letters and reports it would appear that the pope did not finally decide to establish a second rite in America until the first part of 1906. In August and September of 1905, the apostolic delegate asked the American bishops to give him a statistical report on the number of Greek Catholics living in their dioceses.[57] No doubt the total number of Greek Catholics was to be a factor in the pope's decision on a bishop. The Latin bishops responded by reporting very low figures. For example, the bishop of Pittsburgh reported that he had only 15,000 Greek Catholics in his diocese, while Hodobay's statistics indicated that there were 58,000 Greek Catholics in that diocese. Hodobay also inquired of the Greek Catholic pastors in the various dioceses and discovered that none of them had been asked for a census of their congregations. The situation was similar in most of the dioceses, and Hodobay realized the effect such figures could have on the pope's decision. So he documented some of the contradictions and asked the apostolic delegate to sanction an accurate count.[58]

In May 1906, Hodobay reported to the Greek Catholic bishop, John Valyi of Prešov, that the apostolic delegate had informed him that the pope had decided to appoint a bishop for the Greek Catholics in the United States. But Hodobay also heard from Rev. Holoshnay that the apostolic delegate had asked the Greek Catholic priests to make a recommendation.[59] At the same time, Hodobay requested permission from the apostolic delegate to resign his position as apostolic visitor.[60] The resignation would have increased the urgency for the appointment of a bishop and would have increased the pope's dependence on the Hungarian government in making the final choice. The pope was not to be hurried and he never accepted Hodobay's request to resign.

In June 1906, Hodobay reported to the Hungarian government that the Sacred Congregation in Rome had informed him that the Greek Catholic priests in the United States had requested the appointment of a bishop who was an American citizen with no connection to the Hungarian government. Hodobay expressed surprise at this turn of events. But he reported that with these parameters, he would nominate Rev. John Korotnoki of Allegheny who was by this time an American citizen.[61]

Hodobay did not report that Rev. Korotnoki had been sent to America by the Hungarian government and was receiving $1,600 a year in direct subsidy from the Hungarian government.[62] Thus Korotnoki would not have fulfilled the requirement that the nominee be independent of the Hungarian government.

In the spring of 1906, it became obvious to Hodobay and the Hungarian government that they were now competing with the Greek Catholic priests in the United States for the right to nominate the bishop. Hodobay, therefore, wrote a letter to the apostolic delegate reporting that as early as last December, Rev. Alexander Dzubay and Rev. Joseph Hanulya had attempted to organize a congress of all eighty-two Greek Catholic priests in the United States. That congress was canceled because of inadequate preparation.[63] Preparation was necessary since such a congress was opposed by the Latin bishops, and the priests were divided between pro-Ukrainians from Galicia and Hungarians. The Hungarian priests were divided between pro-Magyar and Rusyn-oriented or nationalistic priests. In the spring of 1906 Dzubay and Hanulya planned another congress for the Greek Catholic priests, and this time they requested and received permission from the apostolic delegate with the limitation that they restrict their discussion to their recommendation for a Greek Catholic bishop.[64]

Hodobay was not aware of this permission when he wrote to the delegate that he was "receiving many letters from the Greek Catholic Priests, even from the laity, that I shall make a report immediately to your Excellency and request your Grace to prohibit the Congress in the strongest manner."[65]

The Austro-Hungarian ambassador to Washington was also concerned that the Pope might accept the nomination of the priests rather than that of the Hungarian government. He therefore, wrote an official letter to the apostolic delegate. In the letter the ambassador indicated that his government was interested in the selection of a bishop. His stated reason was that a Greek Catholic bishop would help the Greek Catholics adhere to their creed and prevent them from joining the Orthodox church. The remainder of his letter, however, indicated that his reasons were entirely political; his primary intent was to argue against the priests' nomination of one of their own.[66]

In the letter he observed that the priests wished to support the bishop from funds raised by the congregations. For this purpose they had pledged $4,000 a year. While the ambassador recognized that this method was normally used in the United States, it would not be "conducive to the dignity and independence of the new bishop." It would "be fraught with grave danger" because of the division in the church. The divisions "arise from national feelings and political agitations peculiar to the race and creed of the Greek Catholic immigrants." The ambassador then suggested that the dignity of the bishop's position would be better safeguarded if he were independent of the material contributions of his parishioners and if the readiness of the Hungarian government to contribute to his maintenance would be accepted.[67]

The apostolic delegate's reply was direct and noncommittal; he wrote the ambassador that the Holy Father had indeed decided to give the Greek Catholics their own bishop. He had instructed the apostolic delegate to inquire if the people could support one and if there was anyone from among them who was qualified to fill that position. Beyond that the pope was determined to make his own decision.[68]

In July of 1906, the Hungarian government was deciding who its candidate for American bishop should be. Hodobay seemed to be the first choice. But Hodobay, in a letter to the Hungarian prime minister, indicated in unequivocal terms that he did not want to be a candidate for bishop. He wished to be released of his duty so he could return home.[69]

The Hungarian government finally decided to support the candidacy of Rev. John Korotnoki, the priest from Allegheny, Pennsylvania, who had been receiving a subsidy from the Hungarian government since his arrival in 1902. In January 1907, Ambassador Hengelmuller reported to the Austro-Hungarian foreign minister, Count Aloys Lexa Van Aehrenthal, that Hodobay had formally submitted the name of Korotnoki to the pope as his recommendation for the position of Greek Catholic bishop in America.[70]

In January and February 1907, it was obvious that Rome had all the information needed. The decision now rested with the Sacred Congregation for the Propagation of the Faith to make its recommendation to the pope. Consequently, the Hungarian government's political maneuvering moved from the United States to Rome. The key person there was Count Szecsenyi, ambassador to the Holy See from Austria-Hungary. In early February, Count Szecsenyi reported to Von Aehrenthal that Gotti, the cardinal-prefect of the Sacred Congregation for the Propagation of the Faith, had informed him that a bishop for America would be chosen before the end of the month.[71]

In another account to Von Aehrenthal, Count Szecsenyi reported on another meeting with Cardinal Gotti. Szecsenyi had suggested that of the three candidates for bishop, the pope should choose one from the Munkacs (Mukachevo) or Eperjes (Prešov) dioceses. Gotti responded that they would choose the best qualified of the three. Szecsenyi then reminded the prefect that the vast majority of the Greek Catholics in the United States came from Hungary and therefore, if at all possible, the bishop should be from Hungary. Szecsenyi also suggested that it was very important that the candidate be loyal to the dynasty and the state. Cardinal Gotti assured Szecsenyi that he understood that view and he hoped they could comply with those wishes in making the selection.[72]

That interchange between Szecsenyi and Gotti contains the first and only direct suggestion to the church leaders that they consider Hungarian or state political factors in the selection of the bishop. In the correspondence to that point, political considerations were always hidden in ecclesiastical terminology.

The Gotti-Szecsenyi conversation also suggested that there were three final candidates for American bishop: One was certainly Korotnoki; another was, no doubt, Peter Stefan Soter Ortyns'kyi, who was the one finally selected; and the third was evidently Von Dr. Suba, a Hungarian mentioned by Szecsenyi in a following communication.[73] The fact that the three finalists did not include the choice of the American priests meant that the pope had not given their selection the serious consideration Hodobay and Hengelmuller had feared.[74]

On 19 February Szecsenyi talked with Cardinal Cassetta, another member of the Sacred Congregation. Cassetta was not sympathetic to Szecsenyi's suggestion that a Hungarian be chosen as bishop. Cassetta said that he understood Szecsenyi's position, but he felt that Rev. Korotnoki was not a good candidate because he was involved in the controversy in America. Von Dr. Suba, the other Hungarian candidate, could not speak English and therefore he too was not such a good choice.[75]

Finally, on 28 February 1907, Szecsenyi telegraphed Von

Aehrenthal that the pope had selected a Basilian monk from Lemberg (Lviv) in Galicia named Peter Stefan Soter Ortyns'kyi to be the first Greek Catholic bishop in the United States.[76] That telegram, which was relayed to Dr. Alexander Wekerle, the Hungarian prime minister, signaled the defeat of Hungarian efforts to build a base in America from which to persuade the Rusyn immigrants to adopt the Magyar ideals they had resisted in their homeland. It was perhaps an impossible task at the outset, but it was, nevertheless, a task into which the Hungarian government placed a significant amount of resources.

On 8 March 1907, Cardinal Gotti sent Rev. Hodobay an official notice terminating his tenure as apostolic visitor to the "Ruthenian" rite in America and instructing him to return to Hungary.[77]

5

Conflicts in the Establishment of the Greek Catholic Church in America

The establishment of the Greek Catholic church in America has been studied by many historians and it is virtually always discussed in the context of the Rusyns' conversion to Russian Orthodoxy. The Russian Orthodox church was established in the United States before the Greek Catholic rite was established. The Russian Orthodox church was established among the Rusyns in America in 1891 when St. Mary's Greek Catholic Church of Minneapolis was accepted into the Russian Orthodox church by the Holy Synod. The Greek Catholic "rite" was not established in the United States until 1907 when Pope Leo XIII appointed Soter Ortyns'kyi as its first bishop.

The implication is this: If the Greek Catholic church had been established in America when the Rusyns first came, the Russian Orthodox church would have remained centered in Alaska, or at least would have posed no serious challenge to the Greek Catholic church. The question most historians answer one way or another is: "Who was responsible for the American Catholic church's loss of over one-third of its Rusyns to Orthodoxy?"

The American Latin bishops are the first on the list of those who are blamed.[1] It is not only Greek Catholic historians who blame the bishops; in fact, Greek Catholic historians may even suggest that part of the conflict was a "misunderstanding."[2] Roman Catholic historians are often even more critical of the Latin bishops when discussing Bishop Ireland's "vendetta against the Uniates"[3] which had "dire results for the Church."[4]

In one way or another most historians writing on this topic also blame the laymen, the Rusyns who came to the United States by the tens of thousands. For example: "A few of the 'civic leaders', . . . stubbornly resisted the orders of the Apostolic See."[5]

Hungarian officials blamed the Greek Catholic pastors. These

government strategists felt that the lay people were docile followers of the priests.[6] Occasionally papal decrees, especially
those altering the traditional practices of the "rite," are seen as a
part of the problem.[7] In some cases, especially after the appointment of a Ukrainian bishop, the Ukrainian movement is seen as
divisive.[8]

The whole question is seldom placed in a neutral perspective.
Examining the question of "blame" is not a productive approach
to the study of these conversions. The Rusyns who migrated to a
new world literally entered a new age. The main factors applying
to this situation were freedom, democracy, and separation of
church and state. In the old world, the state provided the church
with the finances through compulsory tax collections. The state
also exerted coercive power to help the church maintain its
position (note the Becherov incident in the previous chapter).

In the United States lack of government support for the
churches did not hamper the development of churches among
the Rusyns. They wanted their churches, so coercive force was
not necessary to keep them faithful. The church provided a
meaningful foundation for their communities.

The new environment in the new world required a new organizational structure for the church. When the Rusyns came to the
United States, there was no church for them. In an ad hoc manner
Rusyn laymen built their own churches and formed their own
congregations. These laymen wished to influence the development of their "creation." The dispute over church organization
developed when traditional church and governmental authorities wished to impose their organizational structures on the
laymen's creation.

Organizational structures require goals and theoretical foundations. Every group that has been blamed for the Rusyns' "problems" had their own goals and theoretical systems. Most of these
goals in some way treated the Rusyns' mundane desires as secondary to the "larger goal." In fact, the favorite villains, the Latin
bishops, made that perspective explicit. At a meeting in Chicago
in 1893, the American archbishops resolved to impose their
standards on the Greek rite, "because the possible loss of a few
souls of the Greek rite, bears no proportion to the blessings
resulting from uniformity of discipline."[9]

Some of the principals in the competition for souls thought
they could use coercion to gain their objectives. However, many
of the forms of coercion (which were effective in Europe) were
not effective in the United States where membership was volun-

tary and the state would not intervene. The Catholic hierarchy, whether Latin or Greek, had difficulty recognizing that fact. (The "Americanist" bishops led by Archbishop Ireland, tried to impress the pope with that fact for many years.)

Some means of control existed in the United States that did not exist in Europe. For example, lay ownership of local church property often gave the congregation power to choose or dismiss its pastor and to ignore the direct orders of Latin and Greek bishops.[10] Such lay power could not have existed in the Rusyn homeland. Misunderstanding is not an accurate term to use when discussing these conflicts over the Rusyn soul since the long-term goals and objectives of the competing factions were often incompatible.

The Russian government and the Orthodox church were just beginning to develop their own interest in the Rusyns. However, Russia had one advantage over the other competitors for the Rusyn soul: Russia, in both its state and church form, knew it had no coercive powers over the Rusyns in either Eastern Europe or in the United States. Therefore its methods had to be the methods of the new world and the new age. Freedom, democratic choice, voluntary association—these were the values Father Alexis Toth represented and these were the values Archbishop Tikhon suggested must be the foundation of a multiethnic Orthodox church in America.[11]

In this context, the Russian Orthodox church provided a positive voluntary option to the acrimonious infighting that existed in the rest of the Rusyn community. Furthermore it was entirely possible for an illiterate Rusyn immigrant to join a local congregation that had the "look and feel" of the church back home and yet that congregation could be a member of the Orthodox church. In other words, it was possible for the Orthodox church to provide the familiar "comfort" the Rusyn immigrant expected from his parish.

In this context it is also useful to evaluate the role of the lay organizations. The Greek Catholic Union was the most significant lay organization for the Subcarpathians. For the Galicians the leading lay organization would have been the Ukrainian National Association and for both Galicians and Subcarpathians who identified themselves as Russian, the Russian Brotherhood Organization was the significant lay organization.

The Ukrainian National Association supported the newly established Greek Catholic church under the leadership of Bishop Ortyns'kyi even when the accompanying papal decree, Ea Semper, required that the bishop alter some of the traditional practices of the Greek Catholic church. The Ukrainian National Association ran afoul of the bishop and developed an adversary relationship with him only after he tried to place the Association under his control, attempting to end its lay autonomy.[12]

The Galician (Ukrainian) lay response to *Ea Semper,* while critical, was probably more accepting of the papal decree than the Subcarpathian response (which must be described as belligerent) because the Galicians were able to find an acceptable identity in the Ukrainian movement. Identification with familiar church traditions was essential for the Subcarpathians because the Subcarpathian Rusyns had only the consistency of church traditions to provide a sense of continuity with their forebears. For that reason the Greek Catholic Union fought rather vigorously to maintain the traditions of the Greek Catholic church with all its familiar details. In so doing it represented the rather strongly held position of most of the Subcarpathian Rusyn immigrants.

An analysis of Orthodox church statistics would suggest that after 1907, it was Rome that must accept responsibility for forcing the Rusyns to make a choice between altered traditions and the Orthodox option. Prior to 1907, a greater percentage of the Rusyns who converted to Orthodoxy came from Galicia, probably indicating that the Subcarpathians had more faith in their community's ability to defend its traditions. After 1907, when the Greek rite was established and the pope had appointed a Galician bishop, most of the conversions to Orthodoxy came from the Subcarpathian Rusyns. The appointment of a Galician bishop was not reassuring to the Subcarpathians, but the accompanying decrees, which the bishop was to enforce, threatened the familiar details of their tradition—details that the Orthodox church left intact.[13]

These statistics weaken somewhat the argument that it was the obstructionism of the Latin rite bishops that forced the Rusyns to turn to Orthodoxy. That observation would not be much comfort for the Catholic church since the responsibility probably shifts from the American bishops to the Roman pontiff and his *Ea Semper* decree.

The pattern for establishing the early Greek Catholic parishes was an unhappy one but one that was repeated over and over again. First came the Rusyn immigrants. They did not feel comfortable in the Latin rite churches so they called a pastor from their Greek Catholic dioceses in Eastern Europe. The first of these was Father John Voliansky who came to Shenandoah, Pennsylvania, in 1884.[14] Sometimes they built a church first and then called a Greek Catholic pastor as was the case in Minneapolis and Wilkes Barre.[15] When the pastors presented themselves to the local Latin rite bishop they were generally rejected because they were married.[16]

These unfortunate encounters between bishop and priest left the Greek Catholic church with no canonical leadership or higher organization. Father Toth and St. Mary's Church in Minneapolis solved their crisis by joining the Russian Orthodox church. This conversion to Orthodoxy required virtually no change in the parishes' traditional practices.[17] Many congregations, clustered together in Pennsylvania, New Jersey, and New York, sought to maintain the Greek Catholic rite in America by maintaining close ties with the bishops in their homeland. These Greek Catholic congregations had no regular standing in the Catholic church.

To correct this problem the Sacred Congregation for the Propagation of the Faith, in 1902, authorized Bishop John Valyi of Prešov to appoint an apostolic visitor to inspect the situation in America and recommend a solution to the problem.[18] Bishop Valyi chose Father Andrew Hodobay to make that inspection.

The Greek Catholic priests, and occasionally the apostolic visitor, Father Hodobay, did have some valid criticisms of some of the Latin bishops. Other nationality groups also shared these complaints. Cardinal John McCloskey of New York is said to have rejected a Polish community's request for its own church by remarking that what the Poles needed was a pig sty.[19]

The German Catholics also vigorously opposed the American "Irish" bishops. Most German Catholic immigrants felt that the American Catholic hierarchy wished to destroy their German heritage. In the early 1890s a German, Peter Paul Cahensly, expressed this German response to the American Catholic hierarchy in his Lucerne Memorial to the pope. He charged that the insensitive Irish bishops had caused over 10 million Catholic immigrants to turn away from the church.[20] The problem may not have been as extreme as Cahensly charged, but the German Catholic immigrants were not afforded entirely equal treatment and the church was unnecessarily "Irish-American" in its treatment of these immigrants.[21]

The Greek Catholic priests could also provide many examples where the bishops refused to cooperate with the priests even when the priests sought to cooperate with them. On one occasion

Rev. Hodobay sent the Greek Catholic priest, Father John Olshaveskii, to Salem, Massachusetts, but the bishop of Boston refused to give him faculties, the authorization to function as a priest. Hodobay complained of this refusal to Archbishop Diomede Flaconio, the apostolic delegate in Washington,[22] who instructed the bishop to grant Olshaveskii the faculties.[23] The bishop obeyed only to the letter of the delegate's orders and granted Olshaveskii faculties for only three days.[24] Falcanio again ordered the bishop to grant Olshaveskii the necessary credentials and instructed Hodobay to again send Olshaveskii to see the bishop for his response.[25]

Olshaveskii finally wrote to Hodobay that he had been to see the bishop six times and had been insulted and ordered out of the office on all occasions.[26] Olshaveskii indicated that the bishop would never give him faculties and would protest contrary orders all the way to Rome. He conceded that part of the bishop's opposition was because the congregation owned the church. The bishop finally ordered Olshaveskii to leave the parish and suggested that the parishioners could be given a Polish priest. However, Olshaveskii observed, "they hate the Polish Priests" and the people would join the Orthodox church first.[27] Not all of the bishops were as uncooperative as the archbishop of Boston but many of the priests empathized with the plight of Olshaveskii and felt that the bishops were at fault.

The bishops, however, saw the problem from the other side. They alleged that there were Greek Catholic priests who were simonists, drunkards, and disobedient without cause. Bishop Eugene Garvey of Altoona was, by all evidence, a good bishop and one who did not wish to destroy the Greek Catholic rite. He cooperated with Hodobay and supported the plan for a separate Greek Catholic bishop in the United States. He wrote to the apostolic delegate that the sooner one was appointed the better.[28] But he too complained about a priest, Rev. Julius Csucska, from whom the bishop had revoked his faculties. When Csucska apologized, Garvey returned them. However Garvey did not have a high opinion of Csucska. Father Csucska had jurisdiction over South Fork as well as his own parish in Johnstown. The Greek Catholics of South Fork wanted to form their own parish and call their own priest. Father Csucska opposed this division, but the bishop felt Csucska was motivated by greed since the two communities were too large for one priest.[29] Hodobay agreed with Garvey that such complaints were made regularly by the bishops, many of which were justified, and that he would forward them to the committee of bishops in Hungary.[30]

Bishop Garvey also had another bad experience with Michael Balogh. Rev. Balogh had performed a baptism for a Mr. Prince. Mr. Prince had paid for the baptism and received a certificate of baptism but Rev. Balogh had failed to sign it and later refused to do so (no reason was indicated in the correspondence). Mr. Prince appealed to Bishop Garvey who ordered Rev. Balogh to sign the certificate but the priest refused.[31] Hodobay recommended that Bishop Garvey suspend the disobedient priest. But Garvey responded that such a course would not help matters because he had no priest to replace Balogh and:

> In all probability his congregation will support him against any "Irish Latin Bishops." I cannot close the church against them since they are the owners and they would probably laugh at an interdict. Men like Balogh know that they have an advantage over the Bishop which no latin priest possesses.[32]

In the above letter, Bishop Garvey succinctly described the plight of many bishops who seriously tried to work with the Greek Catholic priests. As long as the congregation supported their priests, the bishop was helpless to enforce even a simple act such as the signing of a baptismal certificate.

The bishop of Erie, John Fitzmaurice, also cooperated with Hodobay, but he also had some bad experiences with Greek Catholic priests. In 1906, he granted faculties to the priest whom Hodobay had suggested be sent to Hawk Run, Pennsylvania, but the bishop wrote to Hodobay, "I suppose he too will run away as soon as he can like the others." The bishop then complained that he could not see how the bishop of "Eperies" (Prešov) could claim any right over the priests in this country, "if he is a priest in my Diocese, I alone have authority over him."[33]

Sometimes the priests were extreme in their misconduct; but, since there were more congregations than priests, some congregations would hold onto their priests even when there were serious charges against them. Such was the case with Father Volanskii of Bradenville, Pennsylvania. His bishop revoked his faculties because of complaints against him from the congregation. Hodobay investigated the complaints and found that Rev. Volanskii had been imprisoned five times for improper conduct associated with drunkenness. He had often been drunk during Mass and on one occasion had spilled the sacramental wine. He often abused members of the congregation. The list of verified complaints against him was lengthy, but apparently the congregation refused to give him up because they could not get another.[34]

These examples were extreme cases that show the total inability of the bishops to cope with the most blatant infractions of discipline and law. There are other cases of insubordination that suggest that the priests themselves had a loosely knit organization that sometimes infringed on the normal responsibilities of the bishops.

In the fall of 1906 the Rev. Igor Burik moved from a pastorate in the Columbus diocese to St. John the Baptist Church in the Cleveland diocese. St. John's congregation had just "put out" their previous pastor and on the recommendation of Rev. Joseph Hanulya, the congregation called Rev. Burik who accepted.[35] The problem was that neither bishop approved of the move and Hodobay had also opposed it. The bishop of Cleveland suspended Burik and requested that the bishop of Prešov recall him to Hungary, but to no avail.[36]

Joseph Hanulya's recommendation in this matter was significant if not decisive. Hanulya was one of the leaders among the Greek Catholic pastors in the United States. It was Rev. Hanulya and Rev. Dzubay who early in 1906 had called a congress of the Greek Catholic priests to discuss the selection of a bishop.[37] Rev. Hanulya and Rev. Dzubay, while priests of equal rank with the other priests, were recognized as leaders and their recommendations often carried authority normally reserved for a bishop.

The Latin bishops were in a difficult position. They were responsible for the behavior of the Greek Catholic priests in their dioceses but they were virtually helpless to control them. Faced with these realities, it is understandable why some of the bishops refused to cooperate in any way with the priests of the Greek Catholic rite. The system of church organization and authority as the bishops understood it just did not work when applied to a second rite whose congregations and priests felt that they alone were the protectors of their familiar faith in a strange country.

By 1906, the bishops realized they could not force the Greek Catholic congregations to be Latinized, nor could they enforce discipline on the Greek Catholic priests. Bishop Ireland had followed that rigid policy with Father Toth and St. Mary's congregation in Minneapolis in 1890. That congregation converted to

Orthodoxy and was followed by dozens of other congregations in succeeding years. The more perceptive bishops reconsidered their policy and recognized that the Greek Catholics were of a different rite and must be treated differently.

By 1906, Archbishop Ireland was one of these bishops who had reconsidered his policy. In that year he had the opportunity to react to the formation of another Greek Catholic church in his diocese. In the fall of 1906 Rev. Hodobay visited Minneapolis and found that there were a number of Greek Catholic families who had not joined St. Mary's Russian Orthodox Church and who wished to organize their own Greek Catholic congregation.[38]

Hodobay wrote to the Hungarian prime minister recommending that a congregation be established in Minneapolis and that the Hungarian government contribute to the support of a priest there for the first three years. He also requested that the Hungarian government support a cantor because the Russian church had such a beautiful choir that the music alone could entice the Greek Catholics to join the Orthodox.[39]

Hodobay also wrote to Archbishop Ireland requesting his permission to establish a Greek Catholic parish in his diocese. On 31 December 1906, Ireland, gave a very favorable response. He wrote:

> I shall be very glad to see a good priest of the Greek Rite established in Minneapolis. I will cooperate with him to the best of my ability to make his mission a success. Of course you easily understand that the priest coming to Minneapolis must be celibate. The presence of any other would be the occasion of great scandal . . . and I should feel obligated to protest against it.[40]

With the exception of the issue of celibacy, Bishop Ireland had changed his attitude consderably in the last sixteen years since he had expelled Father Toth and ordered St. Mary's congregation to join the Polish congregation nearby.

The Hungarian government was apparently willing to support a priest in Minneapolis even though he would have been "non-Hungarian speaking."[41] However, by the end of February 1907, the pope chose a Galician-Rusyn to be the Greek Catholic bishop in America and the Hungarian government abandoned its support for non-Magyar parishes in the United States.[42] St. John the Baptist Greek Catholic Church of Minneapolis was organized without Hungarian aid.

Even though many of the bishops became reconciled to the

existence of a second rite in the United States as Ireland's letter suggests, they did not accept all the practices of that rite. The bishops most vigorously opposed the right of the Greek Catholic priests to be married. Thus the Greek Catholic priests felt that they must always be on their guard to defend the prerogatives of their rite. In those circumstances, they could not respect the Latin bishops as their legitimate authorities but viewed them as enemies of their rite and of the practices of that rite.

The Rusyn priests, however, were somewhat at a disadvantage. They were not organized. They did not meet together on any regular basis. In 1893 the apostolic delegate had called a meeting of all Rusyn priests to draft a petition requesting that the pope appoint a bishop for them.[43] In December 1905, Rev. Dzubay and Rev. Hanulya attempted to organize a congress of all eighty-two Greek Catholic priests in the United States, but pressure from Latin bishops and disagreement among the priests themselves caused the organizers to cancel the congress.[44] The apostolic visitor, Hodobay, also strongly opposed that meeting. Dzubay and Hanulya proceeded to organize another congress with better preparation. In March 1906, the priests petitioned Archbishop Falconio, the apostolic delegate in Washington, requesting his permission to hold such a congress. The apostolic delegate granted that request but specifically limited the congress's business to the drafting of a petition concerning the future bishop.[45]

The limitation was probably placed on the conference because the Latin rite leadership did not want the Greek Catholic priests to discuss a more permanent organization. Such an organization would more seriously undermine the authority of the Latin rite by providing the priests with a cohesive organization that could provide a united front in the protection of the Greek Catholic rite.

There were also major internal divisions among the priests that hindered establishing a single organization. First of all, there was the division caused by the differing views of national identity between the Rusyns from Galicia and the Rusyns from Subcarpathia. The Galicians, in the first decade of the century, increasingly identified with the Ukrainian movement while the Subcarpathians were hostile to such an identity.[46] In 1906, there were only twenty-one priests from Galicia while there were fifty-nine priests from Northern Hungary.[47] However, the Hungarian priests were also divided among those who were Magyarized and those who were critical of Magyarization.

It is difficult to determine what percentage of priests were on either side of the Magyarization controversy, but Hodobay feared they did not share his Magyar zeal so he opposed their attempts at organization. In a letter to the apostolic delegate in March 1906, Hodobay requested the apostolic delegate to "prohibit the congress in the strongest manner" and to "request the Most Reverend Archbishops and Right Reverend Bishops to inform the Greek Catholic Priests of their Dioceses, that not one shall take part in the congress."[48] But the apostolic delegate had already granted Dzubay and Hanulya permission for the congress. Hodobay "with sorrow" noted that the congress overwhelmingly recommended four priests to be considered for appointment as bishop and, among the four, Father Dzubay was considered. None of the recommended priests were pro-Magyar[49] (but they may not have been anti-Magyar either).

The Greek Catholic priests were never able to organize and become a unified force for the protection of the Greek Catholic rite. It was, therefore, the lay organization, the Greek Catholic Union, that became the strongest unifying agency among the Greek Catholics from Northern Hungary. It was this organization that remained in the forefront in the struggle to protect the privileges of the Greek Catholic rite from encroachment by the Latin rite hierarchy.

The parishes were the second stronghold of lay authority in the Greek Catholic church. The strength of the parishes arose from the fact that, in most cases, a lay board owned the church property.[50] In owning the churches, they adopted the policy of calling and firing their own pastors.[51] The parishes used their independence to determine which policies of the Latin bishops they would follow or reject and, as important, which policies they would allow their pastors to follow.

This parish orientation gave the pastors a certain amount of independence. For example, Rev. Kovaliczkii was asked by the Latin bishops to leave his diocese, and the apostolic delegate asked Hodobay to have the bishop of Prešov recall Kovaliczkii to his original diocese in Hungary. In response, Kovaliczkii told Hodobay that he would not return even if he were threatened with excommunication.[52] No doubt the reason for Rev. Kovaliczkii's boldness was his confidence in his position with his congregation.

It was ironic, in view of the real power the laity possessed, that the bishop of Harrisburg wrote to Hodobay in 1906: "the laity are as, good as they can be. But, oh! they are dreadfully confused and misled by the many priests who are coming to these shores."[53] In some cases the laity were misled by their priests but the laity held the ultimate power in the American Greek Catholic church and the Greek Catholic Union did much to inform and lead the laity.

Church leaders and their apologists have often been critical of this lay "trusteeship" of church property.[54] Church leaders were also critical of the leadership of the Greek Catholic Union and the role it played in informing and leading the lay members of the rite.[55]

To judge the laity and lay organizations fairly, one must use the perspective of the pre-World War I years. The Rusyn Greek Catholic laymen came to the United States before the establishment of the Greek Catholic church. When they came, they had no priests and no churches. As they demonstrated again and again, they would rather become Russian Orthodox than join a Latin rite church.[56] Obviously the more visible aspects of their rite were more important to them than the theological abstraction concerning their churches' highest authority. These laymen built their own churches and to do so they had to own their own property since there was no bishop. Certainly the Latin bishops would not have built a church for them so they could worship in their own traditional way. These laymen were of necessity independent; they even had to call their own pastors from "the old country."[57]

The basic motivating factor that founded and built the Greek Catholic rite in this country was the commitment of the Rusyn immigrant to the practice of his faith. If the Rusyn laymen had not defended the historic privileges of the Greek Catholic rite as practiced in Galicia and Hungary, the rite would never have been established in America.

The basic defense the Rusyns had against the bishops' attempts to Latinize them was their ownership of their churches. As mentioned earlier, the bishops, the priests, and the laymen all recognized that source of power. Rev. Olshaveskii of Salem wrote that the bishops would never grant him faculties "because the Greek united people of Salem is [sic] the owner of the church, etc."[58] He further observed that the 700 Rusyns in the area around Salem "should be schismatic [join the Orthodox church] if privated [sic] of a priest of Greek Catholic Religion (because they hate the Polish Priests)."[59]

As previously mentioned, when Bishop Garvey of Altoona complained about the Greek Catholic priest who refused to sign a baptismal certificate, he indicated that he could not suspend the priest since the congregation owned the church and would ignore an interdict.[60] The power of lay ownership of the parish churches was obvious to all parties. This power was on occasion abused.[61] However, the "trustee system" was the only mechanism that saved the fledgling Greek Catholic churches from absorption by the Latin rite or assimilation by the Orthodox church.

The Rusyn laymen held onto their property because that was the only way they could protect their rite. When they converted to Russian Orthodoxy, they were obligated to sign their property over to the Russian bishop. They were probably willing to do this because they could be confident their traditions would be protected. In fact with only a few exceptions, the parish property in the Russian Orthodox church was owned by the bishop.[62] Thus it is reasonable to conclude that the Rusyns held title to their parish property primarily to safeguard their traditions, not for obstructionist purposes.

At its general meeting in March 1904, the Greek Catholic Union took positive steps to make the union more sensitive to its American environment. One of the resolutions that was passed required all the high officials of the union to be American citizens.[63] Rev. Korotnoki sent a report of this convention to the Austro-Hungarian consul general in Philadelphia. In this report he suggested that this citizenship requirement was very destructive to the Hungarian cause of Magyarizing the Rusyns in America.[64]

It was the Greek Catholic Union that organized the Executive Committee headed by Fathers Hanulya and Dzubay, which petitioned the apostolic delegate for permission to hold a meeting of all the Greek Catholic priests in 1906, to aid in the selection of a bishop.[65] When the Greek Catholic pastors met in New York in March 1906, they also followed the lead of the union and recommended that Rome appoint an American citizen as the Greek Catholic bishop for the United States.[66]

The Greek Catholic Union and its official newspaper, the *Amerikansky Russky Viestnik*, also represented the Rusyns in the area of ethnic awareness. The same organization that led the community in its adaptation to American life also led the community in its attempts to preserve its own ethnic consciousness.

In 1906, while the Greek Catholic priests were requesting an American citizen for a bishop, Rev. Hodobay asked the Hungarian prime minister to influence the pope to select a Hungarian bishop and to send "patriotic priests" who would lead people closer to the Hungarian government.[67] At the same time, the

Greek Catholic Union was planning an ethnic awareness campaign. It is difficult to be more specific about the purpose of the campaign because the principals were not too clear about their own objectives. The campaign, at least in part, was an anti-Magyar campaign.

The 1906 general convention of the union voted to establish a "National Fund." This fund would be financed by taking one cent per month from the individual member's dues. The money would be spent in support of the "national" press in America and Hungary. Each Rusyn parish in Hungary would receive a copy of Amerikansky Russky Viestnik, the union's paper, and the Greek Catholic Union would support Nauka, the Rusyn newspaper in Uzhhorod, Hungary, by purchasing 400 subscriptions per year.[68]

The bishops of Prešov and Mukachaevo were opposed to such distribution of the Viestnik in their dioceses, but a year later both indicated that their parishes did not seem to be getting the Viestnik so perhaps it would not be necessary to organize a campaign against it.[69]

By 1908, Rev. Korotnoki reported that the priests who represent the interests of the Hungarian government "are fully excluded from the organization [Greek Catholic Union]."[70] It is difficult to evaluate the union's objectives in its campaign to develop a closer identification between the Rusyns in Hungary and America, but it certainly ran counter to the Hungarian efforts to Magyarize the Rusyns in both places.

Perhaps the Slovak "Memorial" (Request) to the Hungarian delegate to the Peace Congress in St. Louis best described the attitudes that were developing among the Rusyn immigrants in America. This memorial was signed by a number of Slovak leaders, but also by the president of the Greek Catholic Union and by the editor of Amerikansky Russky Viestnik. They suggested that the Slovak (also Rusyn) immigrant to the United States "takes pride in his american citizenship." "The government of this country does not meddle with the people's customs, faith, or language, wisely leaving these things to the natural process of assimilation."[71]

In the minds of the Rusyn immigrants there was no conflict between the concept of developing a Rusyn consciousness and the process of adapting to American life. In fact the development of self-awareness seemed to ease the adaptation to a strange world. The Greek Catholic Union provided the leadership for these adjustments.

The Greek Catholic Union did not separate immigrant life into the secular and the spiritual. It provided the primary leadership the Rusyns received in both areas of their social existence. In the last days of February 1907, the pope made his decision about whom he would appoint as bishop for the Greek Catholic rite in the United States. He did not choose a Hungarian patriot as the Hungarian government had encouraged him to do, and he did not choose an American citizen as the Rusyn priests in America had petitioned. The pope chose Peter Stefan Soter Ortyns'kyi of Galicia as the new bishop.[72]

This choice was a shock, not only to the Hungarian patriots, but also to the Subcarpathian Rusyn immigrant community and to the leaders of the Greek Catholic Union. The Rusyns from northern Hungary were very suspicious of the new bishop. They suspected him of being a "Ukrainian." As a result of these suspicions, the leaders of the Subcarpathian Rusyn community did not cooperate very well with their new bishop.[73]

Conflict over ethnic identity was not the only problem that prevented Bishop Ortyns'kyi from receiving the confidence of the Subcarpathian Rusyn community. Shortly after Ortyns'kyi's appointment, in the fall of 1907, the pope issued a "pastoral letter" defining the restrictions placed on the new bishop. This letter was a further clarification of the *Ea Semper* decree issued by the Sacred Congregation for the Propagation of the Faith in June 1907. Together these two statements reduced Bishop Ortyns'kyi's role to that of an assistant to the Latin bishops in the United States.[74]

Ea Semper severed the jurisdictional ties between the Rusyn pastors in the United States and the bishops in the Old Country, required that all future priests coming to the United States be celibate, and forbade the priests to perform the sacrament of confirmation.[75] However, Bishop Ortyns'kyi also was a Greek Catholic with the same theological heritage as the Subcarpathian Rusyns and he also resented the papal subversion of the rite's historical privileges. So he did not focus on the celibacy instructions and promptly requested Bishop Julius Firczak of Mukachaevo to send two married priests to be placed in Subcarpathian parishes.[76]

The establishment of Rusyn communities in the United States required creative new patterns of organization because the American environment was decidedly different from the Old World environment. Social structure and church organization must be adapted to meet the needs of the people. A church organization that places its own organizational interests over the needs of its members cannot expect the support of those members. In the case of the Rusyns and the establishment of the Greek Catholic church in the United States, the lay people themselves best understood the form the church must adopt in order to serve their needs.

Catholic church authorities in Rome belatedly, and only partially, understood the role of the church among the Rusyn immigrants. The American Catholic church leadership was more interested in preserving an exclusive rite in America than in having the church serve the needs of the Rusyn immigrants. It is very likely that only the competition from the Orthodox church pressured the Latin leaders to rethink their exclusiveness.

The Greek Catholic Union may have been difficult for the church leaders to deal with, especially when they challenged the authority of the union, but the union probably more accurately reflected the needs of the Rusyn community. The Greek Catholic church was finally established, but only grudgingly and only after many of the visible traditions of the rite had been altered to conform to the Latin tradition.

Epilogue: The Fruits of Propaganda and Rivalry

In the early twentieth century the strategists for the Russian and the Austro-Hungarian Empires were interested in cultivating the good will of the general population of the United States. However, prior to the assassination of the Austrian Archduke Ferdinand in June 1914, the primary emphasis was on influencing the immigrants from Eastern Europe. The preceding chapters have examined the attempts and the methods used by the various governments to influence the Rusyn immigrants. Here the focus will be on those governments' attempts to influence the American people on the eve of the Great War.

This campaign to "acquaint" the American people with the interests of the various countries in the maneuvering that preceded the outbreak of the war in 1914 was illustrated by the writing of the Hungarian publicist, Alexander Konta. He wrote that three Hungarian statesmen had been lecturing in the United States for the last two years "to acquaint the American people with the Hungarian cause of Democracy."[1] This "Hungarian cause of Democracy" was an issue that was a purely internal affair within the Austro-Hungarian Empire and could not have been meaningful to many Americans. But in March of 1913 he was able to publish an article in the *New York Times* entitled, "Russia's Conspiracy against Americanizing Aliens."[2] In this article, Konta, a Hungarian immigrant,[3] claimed to have exposed the "real purpose" of the Russian Orthodox mission in America:

Russification is the purpose, not Americanization. Russification by means of religion. . . . In fact Americanization is to be counteracted in every possible way, it seems, since the real service of these converts will not lie in their continued residence in this country, but in their return to the old, where they are to swell the numbers and the influence of the Panslavist campaign for the westward extension of Russian power. . . . It is all for the greater glory, the greater strength of the Czar, for the promotion of Russian's ambitious plans in Eastern Europe.[4]

This article was designed to anger Americans who disliked having foreign powers meddling in American affairs. At that time Russia was also receiving bad press regarding the restrictive foreign travel policy toward Jews. This climate resulted in the United States Senate rejecting a new consular treaty with Russia.

The anti-Russian article did not get any immediate response or follow-up, at least not in the New York Times. The American press did not seem to be willing to go on an anti-Russian campaign even though the news coverage clearly indicated that Russian treatment of the Jews was unpopular. The following year in May 1914, the head of the Russian Orthodox church, Archbishop Platon Rozhdestvenskii, was recalled to Russia and the New York Times carried a very favorable article on his tenure in America.[5] Briefly describing the church's addition of 100 congregations as it grew from West to East, the news article commended Platon for his statesmanship regarding relations between the United States and Russia. The paper reported that Platon had requested that his congregations not participate in any demonstrations that might stir up ill will between the two countries.[6]

In July 1914, just after the assassination of the archduke, the Hungarian parliamentarian, Count Michael Karolyi, made one of several visits to the United States.[7] A New York Times editorial indicated that the Hungarian campaign was only partially successful. The writer observed that Count Karolyi had come at a most opportune time; perhaps he could explain some of the implications of the assassination of the archduke.[8] The editorialist concluded that perhaps Archduke Ferdinand's "Triune Federation" (which was strongly opposed by Hungary) would have been compatible with the ideals of civil liberties for Hungarians as well as the Slavs, who had fewer liberties than the Hungarians in the empire.[9] The Triune Federation would give the three dominant groups—German, Slav, and Hungarian—autonomy based on race rather than territory; the Austrian Germans would resist annexation by Germany and the Slavs would resist annexation by Russia.[10] Events following shortly after that editorial proved that the Triune Federation was not to be, but the general American attitude was probably reflected in that editorial.

In September 1914, after hostilities had begun in Europe, American news reports of domestic affairs turned sharply against the Austrian-German alliance (Central Powers). On 6 September 1914, the front page headlines of the New York Times read: "Dumba The Austro-Hungarian ambassador to the United States

Admits Plot to Cripple Munitions Plants."[11] That article and succeeding coverage indicated that the Austrian ambassador had developed a plan to incite labor strife among the immigrant workers in munitions plants. In the following months the newspapers were filled with reports and rumors of Hungarian, Austrian, and German infiltration into the munitions plants, of Ambassador Dumba's recall at President Wilson's request, and numerous rumors of German plots to blow up munitions plants and bridges. The latter rumors were never substantiated and no instances of bombing were actually reported, but any German-Austrian-Hungarian propaganda campaign to positively influence the American public totally failed within months of the outbreak of the war in 1914.

The Russians, however, continued to gain positive press coverage in the *New York Times*. A traveler to Russia reported less restriction for travelers and more freedom for women there than in Germany or Austria.[12] Other headlines referred to the loyalty of the Slavs to the United States[13] and examples of "Russian Orthodox Church Litany Said in English."[14] In the early years of American neutrality (1914–15), the *New York Times* carried no article challenging the patriotism of Slavs in America.

From 1890 until the First World War, the "Ukrainophiles" and "Muskophiles" were in direct competition seeking to make the Galician Rusyns in America either Ukrainians or Russians. It was also during this period that Russia, through the activities of the Orthodox church and the Slavic societies, increased its efforts to assimilate the Rusyns into Great Russian culture.

In January 1915, the Holy Synod in Petrograd (St. Petersburg) authorized the establishment of the North American Orthodox Brotherhood with the purpose of uniting the dispersed Orthodox in America and Europe with the Russian people.[15]

The wife of the Russian ambassador in Washington organized the Russian-American War Relief Society to collect money and clothing for people in Russian Poland and Galicia.[16] The Russian Club of America was also founded in 1915 for social and intellectual activities, encouragement of the Russian language and culture, and development of "friendly relations between the American people."[17] Honorary members of the club were the tsar of Russia and the president of the United States. (It is unlikely that President Wilson authorized this use of his name prior to American participation in the war.)

American Ukrainian activists observed Russian propaganda activities in America during the war years. They charged that the

"Czarist regime and its spiritual arm, the Orthodox Church" were proselytizing among the Ukrainians by building churches for them in communities where the Ukrainian population was too small for a church or where there was already one Greek Catholic church without resources for another. The Russian Orthodox church in Wilton, North Dakota, was one such example.[18]

Archbishop Evdokim Mischersky who built the Wilton church for seven families in 1916 was evidently responding to the dictates of a wartime public relations campaign rather than the needs of the community. The money for this campaign, however, did not come from Russia. The archbishop raised money by mortgaging other churches and parish houses in the diocese.

The Russian Orthodox church continued an active program to win the allegiance of the Rusyns in America and also to gain the support of the American public in general. One of the most effective propagandists for the Russians was Peter Kohanik. Emigrating from the Carpathians when he was young, he was sent to Russia for his seminary training. He became an active priest in the Russian Orthodox church in the United States. Kohanik wrote a pamphlet entitled *The Austro-German Hypocrisy and the Russian Orthodox Greek Catholic Church*.[19] This was a response to the *New York Times* article by Konta in which Konta charged that the Russian church was "preventing the Americanization of aliens."[20] He concluded that "never has a single Russian person ever been accused of a political crime like the German falsification of citizenship papers and passports."[21] He emphasized that the younger generation attended public schools and spoke English more fluently than "the native tongue."[22]

The pro-Austrian group also published a series of pamphlets in 1915. The ones bearing the most directly on the Rusyn community were published by the Ukrainian National Council in Jersey City.[23] These pamphlets indicate that the leaders of the Ukrainian movement were very pro-Austrian. In all fairness, however, it must be noted that the pro-Austrian position of the Ukrainian movement did not stem from sympathy for Austria so much as it did from hostility toward Russia.

Perhaps the most interesting pamphlet published by the Ukrainian National Council in 1915 was entitled *The Russian Plot to Seize Galicia*. This pamphlet was interesting because it was first published in London in March 1914, before the war broke out. It was basically a prediction of Russia's belligerent intentions in Galicia. When the pamphlet was republished in 1915, numerous clippings of newspaper accounts were added.

These clippings described the Russian occupation of Galicia and generally suggested that the predictions made a year earlier had already been fulfilled. "The Russian plot to seize Galicia" had been successful. The writer now wished to rally support to drive the Russians back out of Galicia.[24]

A pamphlet called *The Ukraine and the Ukrainians* by another leader of the Ukrainian movement, Stefan Rudnitsky, was originally written in German in Vienna in September 1914, and was translated into English for publication in the United States in 1915.[25] The pamphlet contained a survey of the geography, culture, language, race, and history. It cited the importance of the Ukraine, and defended the argument that the Ukraine was a separate nation subjugated by Russia. The maps accompanying the pamphlet showed the Ukrainians occupying an area that, if separated from Russia, would completely cut Russia off from the Black Sea.

The pamphlet concluded with the statement: "Russia has become what she is owing to her possession of the Ukraine; the overwhelming predominnance [sic] of Russia in Europe can only be broken by separating the Ukraine from its connection with the Russian state."[26]

To cut Russia off from the Black Sea and thus remove her from contention in the Balkans and competition for Constantinople would have been the ultimate objective of Austrian foreign policy. This demonstrated how closely the objectives of the Ukrainian movement to establish a separate Ukrainian state fit the objectives of Austrian foreign policy.

This type of propaganda was reasonably effective in the United States. Even after the Austrian espionage reports in the fall of 1914 destroyed popular newspapers' receptiveness to direct Austrian propaganda, the newspapers were still willing to sympathize with suppressed minorities such as the Ukrainians. These papers published articles critical of the Russian treatment of the people in Galicia.

Both the Russians and the Austrians sought to use the Rusyn immigrants in America as vehicles for propaganda. The Russians utilized the Orthodox church structure to improve the Russian image and visibility in the United States and the Austrians encouraged publicity for the Ukrainian movement with its anti-Russian objectives after the American press had rejected more direct Austrian propaganda.

Propaganda is often used by belligerents to keep neutral countries neutral or to persuade neutral countries to become sympathetic to their cause. However, Russian interest in the Rusyns in America seems to have been more far reaching than simple wartime propaganda. As early as 1891, when the first Rusyn Greek Catholic congregation converted to Russian Orthodoxy, the Russian government seems to have felt that the Rusyn population in the United States could have a significant impact on the destinies of the Rusyn population in Eastern Europe. It is interesting then to look at the issue of the influence of the American Rusyn population on the peacemakers in Paris who redrew the map of Eastern Europe in 1919–20.

Historians have maintained that "the Ruthenian immigrants in America did determine the fate of their compatriots at home, a unique case it appears, of the influence on the political history of Europe."[27] More recent research on this question, however, seems to indicate that the earlier historians were too generous; perhaps the immigrant congresses did not have the impact they allegedly had on the postwar destiny of Subcarpathia.[28]

The changing position of the Rusyn immigrants concerning which larger country should contain the autonomous Rusyn area,[29] would suggest that the Rusyn community made a positive response to President Wilson's position rather than Wilson making a positive response to their position. At the peace conference in Paris, Wilson supported the position that Subcarpathia should be annexed to Czechoslovakia.

If there had been no revolutions in Russia in 1917, or even if there had been only one, then perhaps the Russian quest for the Rusyn soul might have been the most brilliant foundation for a successful foreign policy any victorious nation could have brought to the peace table in Paris in 1919. But the Russian Bolshevik Revolution in October–November 1917, wiped out all the carefully laid foundations of the tsarist policy makers.

Bolshevik Russia was not represented at the peace conferences, so the Russian option was never seriously considered for the Rusyns. For that matter the Ukrainian option was also not seriously considered. The Galician Rusyns were placed under the subjugation of the Poles, and the Subcarpathian Rusyns were never granted the autonomy they had been promised within the Czechoslovak state. Eventually the Rusyns in the United States were cut off from the old country by a second world war.

Certainly history has many ironies—the plans of Imperial Russia and the Austrian Empire came to naught. For forty five years after the second world war, the Ukrainian solution to the Rusyn question was accomplished in a geographical sense, but so were

the political objectives of Imperial Russia. The lands of the Rusyns were united with the Ukrainian Republic within the Soviet
Union, a political unit dominated by Russia.

Recent events have again altered the conclusion of this saga.
Perhaps the Ukrainian quest for the Rusyn soul will be successful as the Ukrainian Republic of the Soviet Union emerges as
an Independent Ukrainian State.

Until the changes under the Soviet leader Mikhail Gorbachev,
The Subcarpathian Rusyns in the United States were cut off from
the changes in their homeland. (This observation does not apply
to the Galician Rusyns who have identified with the Ukrainian
movement. American Ukrainians have tenaciously maintained
contacts with Ukrainians in Eastern Europe.) For the most part,
American Rusyns rejected the Soviet solution to the Rusyn question. Some identified themselves as Ukrainians who dreamed of
an independent Ukraine; others still identify themselves as Russians but associate their heritage with that of a prerevolutionary
Russia. Still others, mostly Subcarpathian Rusyns, speak of a
Rusyn nationality born in the Carpathians and reject a broader
definition of their heritage. Indeed the Rusyns have a rich past, a
past that should not be ignored simply because the people and
their lands have been incorporated within a larger political and
geographical area.

Notes

Introduction: The Rusyns

1. Paul Magocsi has made two excellent surveys of these Rusyns. His book *Galicia: A Historical Survey and Bibliographic Guide* (Toronto: University of Toronto Press, 1983) provides an excellent historical and bibliographical survey of the Rusyns in Galicia. His bibliographical analysis identifies works that are of the Russian or Ukrainian perspective. His work, *Shaping a National Identity: Subcarpathian Rus', 1848–1948* (Cambridge: Harvard University Press, 1978) does the same for the Subcarpathians.

2. Oscar Halecki, *From Florence to Brest: 1439–1536* (New York: Fordham University Press, 1958); Basil Boysak, *The Fate of the Holy Union in Carpatho-Ukraine* (Toronto and New York, 1963); Michael Lacko, *The Union of Uzhorod* (Cleveland, Ohio: Slovak Institute, 1976).

3. Robert A. Kann, *A History of the Habsburg Empire 1526–1918* (Berkeley: University of California Press, 1974) examines the Rusyns in Galicia in the larger context of the history of the Habsburg Empire but he is less helpful with an analysis of the Subcarpathians. C. A. Macartney, *The Habsburg Empire, 1790–1918* (New York: Macmillan, 1969) places more emphasis on the Subcarpathians. Robert A. Kann and David V. Zdenek, *The Peoples of the Eastern Habsburg Lands, 1526–1918* (Seattle: University of Washington Press, 1984) use a different approach but more effectively analyze the historical relationship among the non-German peoples of the empire.

4. Athanasius Pekar, *Historic Background of the Eparchy of Prjashev* (Pittsburgh, Pa.: Byzantine Seminary Press, 1968), pp. 3–7.

5. Walter Warzeski, *Byzantine Rite Rusins in Carpatho-Ruthenia and America* (Pittsburgh, Pa.: Byzantine Seminary Press, 1971); and Bohdan P. Procko, *Ukrainian Catholics in America* (Lanham, Md.: University Press of America, 1982).

6. While many Ukrainian historians assume that the terms *Rusyn* and *Ukrainian* are interchangeable, a very significant Polish scholar of nineteenth-century Galicia attempts to support the Rusyn-Ukrainian assertion by demonstrating that the Galician Rusyns identified with Ukrainians in the early nineteenth century. See: Jan Kozik, *Ukrainian National Movement in Galicia: 1815–1849* (Edmonton, Alberta: Canadian Institute of Ukrainian Studies, 1986).

7. Z. A. B. Zeman, *The Breakup of the Habsburg Empire: 1914–1918* (London: Oxford University Press, 1961).

8. See chapter 4 of this study.

9. Marvin R. O'Connell, *John Ireland and the American Catholic Church* (St. Paul: Minnesota Historical Society Press, 1988), pp. 269–71.

10. There are numerous studies that chronicle the divisive tensions within the Habsburg Empire that led to the First World War. One of the best is Zeman, *The Breakup of the Habsburg Empire*. A. J. P. Taylor has a very readable book

dealing with that subject, *The Habsburg Monarchy* (London: Hamish Hamilton, 1966), but his earlier work, which more broadly analyzes the tensions among the nations that led to the war, *The Struggle For Mastery In Europe, 1848–1918* (London: Clarendon Press, 1954; paperback, Oxford University Press, 1977) scarcely mentions the Rusyns by any name.

11. Robert F. Byrnes, *Pobedonostev, His Life and Thought* (Bloomington: Indiana University Press, 1968) provides an excellent analysis of this effort.

12. Byrnes's biography of *Pobedonostsev* documents these Russian interests very well.

13. Robert Paul Magocsi, *Our People: Carpatho-Rusyns and Their Descendants in North America* (Toronto: The Multicultural History Society of Ontario, 1984), pp. 13–15. Magocsi makes a statistical argument that the number of Rusyn immigrants could have been as low as 215,000, but that would not include immigrants who adopted non-Rusyn identifications.

14. Ivan L. Rudnytsky, "Ukrainians in Galicia under Austrian Rule," *Austrian History Yearbook* 3, pt. 2 (1967): 394–429.

15. See chapter 4 of this study.

16. Bohdan P. Procko, *Ukrainian Catholics in America* (Lanham, Md.: University Press of America, 1982).

17. Kahn, *A History of the Habsburg Empire.*

18. Scotus, Viator (R. W. Seton-Watson), *Racial Problems in Hungary* (London: A. Constable & Co., 1908). Seton-Watson was one of the first Western observers to realize that the Magyars were not the innocent, injured nationalists they said they were. He began his journey as a Magyarophile but ended it as an articulate critic of Magyarization.

19. John-Paul Himka, *Socialism in Galicia* (Cambridge: Harvard University Press, 1983); and Kozik, *Ukrainian National Movement.*

20. See chapter 3 of this study.

Chapter 1. The Development of National Awareness among the Rusyns in the Austrian Empire

1. John-Paul Himka, "Priests and Peasants: The Greek Catholic Pastor and the Ukrainian National Movement in Austria, 1867–1900," in *Canadian Slavonic Papers,* 21, no. 1 (Ottawa: Carlton University [Offprint distributed by Harvard University Ukrainian Studies Fund], p. 3.

2. Waclaw Zaleski was one such Polish writer who published a book of peasant songs in 1833. His views are discussed in Kozik, *Ukrainian National Movement,* p. 32ff.

3. Mykhailo Kachkovs'kyi is a good example of a Rusyn civil servant who adopted Polish ways until the 1830s when he decided that he was Rusyn and not Polish. Bogdan Dieditskii, ed., *Mikhail Kachkovskii i sovremennaia galitsko-russkaia literatura* (Mikhail Kachovskii and Contemporary Galician-Russian Literature) (Lviv: Stavropigian Institute, 1876).

4. Kozik, *Ukrainian National Movement,* p. 39ff.

5. Kozik, *Ukrainian National Movement,* p. 59ff.; also Magocsi, *Galicia,* pp. 106–11.

6. Kozik, *Ukrainian National Movement,* p. 59ff; also Magocsi, *Galicia,* pp. 106–11.

7. Kozik, *Ukrainian National Movement*, p. 154.

8. Jan Kozik suggests that Iakiv Holovats'kyi, a member of the Rusyn Triad who eventually emigrated to Russia, concluded in an article published in 1846 under a pseudonym (Havrylo Rusyn) that the Galician Rusyns should not plan to join with the Ukrainians in Russia but rather their destiny would lie with the Austrian monarchy. Kozik, *Ukrainian National Movement*, pp. 167–70.

9. Kozik, *Ukrainian National Movement*, p. 112.

10. Kozik, *Ukrainian National Movement*, p. 114.

11. Ivan Rudnitsky, "The Ukrainians in Galicia under Austrian Rule," in *The Austrian History Yearbook* 3 pt. 2, (Houston, Tex.: Rice University, 1967), p. 399.

12. Dieditskii, *Mikhail Kachkovskii*, pp. 109–10.

13. Dieditskii, *Mikhail Kachkovskii*, pp. 109–10.

14. Dieditskii, *Mikhail Kachkovskii*, pp. 109–10.

15. Dieditskii, *Mikhail Kachkovskii*, pp. 112–13.

16. Ivan Rudnitsky, "Transcarpathia," *Ukraine, A Concise Encyclopedia*, vol. 1 (Toronto: University of Toronto Press, 1963); Magosci, *The Shaping of a National Identity*, pp. 43–47.

17. I. O. Panas, "Karpatorusskiie otzvuki russkago pokhoda v Vengrii 1849 goda," *Karpatorusskii sbornik* (Uzhgorod: Subcarpathian Enlightenment Union, 1930), p. 209.

18. *Pamiati Protoiereia Ioanna Grigorevicha Naumovicha* (In memory of Archpriest Ioann Grigorevich Naumovich) (Odessa: Galician-Russian Benevolent Society, 1912), p. 13.

19. I. O. Panas, "Karpatorusskie otzvuki," p. 210.

20. Dieditskii, *Mikhail Kachkovskii*, pp. 109–10.

21. Dieditskii, *Mikhail Kachkovskii*, pp. 50–54.

22. Stanley B. Kimball, *The Austro-Slav Revival: A Study of Nineteenth Century Literary Foundations* (Philadelphia: The American Philosophical Society, 1973), p. 74.

23. Himka, *Socialism in Galicia*, p. 41.

24. E. Vytanovych, "The Western Ukrainian Lands under Austria and Hungary, 1772–1918," in vol. 1, *Ukraine: A Concise Encyclopedia*, pp. 698–707.

25. Ivan Rudnitsky, "The Ukrainians in Galicia," p. 408.

26. Dieditskii, *Mikhail Kachkovskii*. Most of this summary of Kachkovs'kii's life is taken from this work, which was published by the Stavropigian Institute in 1876 and was a part of the Russian-Galician publication effort of that period.

27. Dieditskii, *Mikhail Kachkovskii*, pp. 50–53.

28. Dieditskii, *Mikhail Kachkovskii*, p. 63.

29. Dieditskii, *Mikhail Kachkovskii*, p. 74.

30. Dieditsdkii, *Mikhail Kachkovskii*, pp. 109–14.

31. Dieditskii, *Mikhail Kachkovskii*, pp. 114–16.

32. By E. A., "Kachkovskii Mikhail Alekseevich," in *Pamiati . . . Naumovicha*, pp. 46–69.

33. Most of the information in this sketch of Ioann Naumovich is taken from a speech honoring the memory of Naumovich and given before the Odessa chapter of the Galician-Russian Benevolent Society in 1912. The speech was given by E. A. (no further identification) and was published in *Pamiati Protoiereia Ioanna Grigorevicha Naumovicha* (Odessa: Galician-Russian Benevolent Society, 1912).

34. *Pamiati . . . Naumovicha,* p. 12.
35. *Pamiata . . . Naumovicha,* p. 13.
36. *Pamiati . . . Naumovicha,* pp. 17–18.
37. *Pamiati . . . Naumovicha,* pp. 24–25; also see Lencyk, "The Ukrainian Catholic Church," p. 187.
38. *Pamaiti . . . Naumovicha,* pp. 25–26.
39. Mieczyslaw Tanty, "Kontaky Rosyjskich Komitetow Slowianskich ze Slowianami z Austro-Wegier," (The Contacts of the Russian Slavic Committees with the Austro-Hungarian Slaves), *Kwartalnik Historyczny* 71, no. 1 (1964): 59–77.
40. *Pamiata . . . Naumovicha,* pp. 26–32.
41. Both Rudnitsky, "The Ukrainians in Galicia," p. 411; and Lencyk, "The Ukrainian Catholic Church since 1800," in *Ukrainian Encyclopedia,* vol. 2 (Toronto: University of Toronto Press, 1971), p. 188, identify the arrests and subsequent prosecution of this group in the early 1880s as the turning point in the conflict between the pro-Russians and the Ukrainophiles.
42. V. A. Frantsev, "Iz istorii bor'by za ruskii literaturnyi iazyk' v' Podkarpatskoi Rusi v polovine XIX St.," in *Karpatorusskii sbornik* (Uzhgorod: PNS, 1930), pp. 6–9.
43. "National'noe dvizhenie v' Ugorskoi Rusi," in *Gelitsko-russkii viestnik,* no. 1 (1894): 52–56.
44. V. A. Frantsev, "Iz istorii bor'by," pp. 6–9.
45. "Natsionalnoe dvizhenie v' Ugorskoi Rusi," pp. 52–53.
46. "Natsionalnoe dvizhenie v' Ugorskoi Rusi," pp. 52–53; and Magocsi, *Shaping of a National Identity,* pp. 47–48.
47. *Karpatorusskii sobornik,* p. 7.
48. *Karpatorusskii sobornik,* p. 7.
49. Published in *Zoria halytska,* no. 39 (1852), as discussed in *Karpatorusskii sbornik,* p. 8.
50. Rudnitsky, "The Ukrainians in Galicia", p. 409.
51. *Karpatorusskii sbornik,* pp. 25–30.
52. *Karpatorusskii sbornik,* pp. 25–30.
53. This generalization is not absolute and does not hold true for the uneducated masses. Many of these, when transplanted to America, developed a "Rusyn" nationalism centered around the Greek Catholic church.
54. Himka, "Priests and Peasants," pp. 5–7.
55. Himka, "Priests and Peasants," pp. 7–14.
56. Himka, *Socialism in Galicia,* p. 167.
57. Himka, *Socialism in Galicia,* p. 167. Also see v. Malanchuk, et al., *L'vivs'ka oblast',* unnumbered volume, *Istoriia mist i sil Ukrains'koi' RSR* (Kiev: AN URSR, 1969), pp. 17–19.
58. Athanasias Pekar, *Historic Background of the Eparchy of Prjashev* (Pittsburgh, Pa.: Byzantine Seminary Press, 1968), pp. 21–33.
59. See chapter 2.
60. John-Paul Himka, "The Ukrainian National Movement before 1914," in Paul Robert Magocsi, *Morality and Reality: The Life and times of Andrei Sheptyts'kyi* (Edmonton, Alberta: Canadian Institute of Ukrainian Studies, 1989), pp. 38–42.

Chapter 2. Russian Interests in the Rusyns in the Austro-Hungarian Empire from 1900 to World War I

1. Historical literature on Pan-Slavism in English is plentiful, if not very recent. Perhaps the best-known work and the broadest in scope is Hans Kohn's *Pan Slavism, Its History and Ideology* (Notre Dame, Ind.: Notre Dame University Press, 1953). But there are other, more detailed studies such as Michael B. Petrovich's work *The Emergence of Russian Pan-Slavism, 1856–1870,* (New York: Columbia University Press, 1956) and some specialized studies such as David Mackenzie's study, *Serbs and Pan-Slavism, 1875–1878* (Ithaca: Cornell University Press, 1956). But perhaps the most balanced account of Pan-Slavism in the English language is Robert F. Byrnes's work *Pobedonostsev, His Life and Thought* (Bloomington: Indiana University Press, 1968). While the title would suggest that the book is merely a biography of Konstantin Pobedonostsev, it also contains an excellent account of Pan-Slavism.

2. For example, Hans Kohn observed that "after the brief war against Turkey, not only the government looked with disfavor upon Pan-Slavism, the great majority of Russian society rejected the nationalist philosophy of slavophilism and its anti-western attitude." Kohn, *Pan Slavism*, p. 170.

3. Robert F. Byrnes makes that point in his study of *Pobedonostsev.*

4. Byrnes, *Pobedonostsev*, p. 211.

5. Byrnes, *Pobedonostsev*, p. 211.

6. Byrnes, *Pobedonostsev*, p. 219.

7. Byrnes, *Pobedonostsev*, p. 225. Byrnes borrowed the term *cultural imperialism* from a work by Theofanis Stavrou, *Russian Interests in Palestine, 1882–1914* (Thessaloniki: Institute for Balkan Studies, 1963).

8. Byrnes, *Pobedonostsev*, p. 218.

9. Victor S. Mamatey has observed that "contrary to a very common belief, most of the irredentisms of the Austrian Empire originated in it, not outside of it. It was the Austrian Slavs who first appealed to Russia, not Russia to them." Victor S. Mamatey, *The United States and East Central Europe, 1914–1918* (Princeton: Princeton University Press, 1957), p. 16.

10. Hans Kohn seems to identify a reemergence of Pan-Slavism with a more traditional concept of imperialism suggesting imperialistic thrust contributed to the causes of the First World War. (Kohn, *Panslavism*).

11. Z. A. B. Zeman supported that point when he wrote:

> The encouragement of refractory nationalist movements in enemy territories was not a game at which any of the European Powers were very skilled at the time of the outbreak of the war. . . . Only in Russia were there signs that the High Command under Grand Duke Nikolai Nikolaevich intended to explore the ground that had been prepared by the activities of men like Count Iurii Bobrinskii—who was appointed the military governor of the Austro-Hungarian territory during the short-lived occupation by the Tsarist Army. . . . The Russians made the first move on the field of political warfare with the Grand Duke's declaration to the nationalities of the Habsburg Empire of 16 September 1914.

Z. A. B. Zeman, *The Breakup of the Habsburg Empire, 1914–1918* (London: Oxford University Press, 1961), p. 65.

12. Mackenzie, *The Serbs and Pan-Slavism.*

13. Rudnitsky. "Ukrainians in Galicia Under Austrian Rule," p. 421.

14. Rudnitsky. "Ukrainians in Galicia Under Austrian Rule," p. 421.

15. Rudnitsky. "Ukrainians in Galicia Under Austrian Rule," pp. 425–26.

16. Rudnitsky. "Ukrainians in Galicia Under Austrian Rule," pp. 425–28.

17. Vladimir Shchavinskii, "Kul'turno-natsional'naia zhizn' Galitskoi Rusi," *Slavianskii viek* (Vienna) no. 83 (14 June 1904), pp. 324–24. (Hereafter *S.viek*)

18. Shchavinskii, "Kul'turno-natsional'naia zhizn' Galitskoi Rusi," p. 325.

19. Shchavinskii, "Kul'turno-natsional'naia zhizn' Galitskoi Rusi," pp. 327–29.

20. Shchavinskii, "Kul'turno-natsional'naia zhizn' Galitskoi Rusi," p. 332.

21. Shchavinskii, "Kul'turno-natsional'naia zhizn' Galitskoi Rusi," p. 332.

22. A news short in *S. viek*, no. 63 (15 Apr. 1903), p. 471.

23. Magocsi, *The Shaping of a National Identity*, pp. 56, 57.

24. *S. viek*, no. 61 (1 Feb. 1903), pp. 407–8.

25. *S. viek*, no. 61 (1 Feb. 1903). On back cover.

26. *S. viek*, no. 61 (1 Feb. 1903). On back cover.

27. D. N. Vergun, *Karpatskie otzvuki* (New York, 1920), from the one-page biography in the introduction.

28. *S. viek*, no. 63 (15 Apr. 1903), p. 469.

29. See *Otchet o dieiatel'nosti Galitsko-russkago Blagotvoritel'nago Obshchestva: 1912* (St. Petersburg: Galitsko-russkago Obshchestva, 1913).

30. Vergun, *Karpats'kie otzvuiki*, p. 54, translated by Dyrud.

31. Vergun, *Karpats'kie otzvuki*, pp. 62–64.

32. Vergun, *Karpats'kie otzvuki*, p. 156.

33. *S. viek*, no. 63 (15 Apr. 1903), p. 469.

34. *S. viek*, no. 64 (1 May 1903), pp. 494–96.

35. *S. viek*, no. 61 (1 Feb. 1903), pp. 407–8.

36. *S. viek*, no. 88 (25 Nov. 1904), p. 485. The transliteration for *Amerikansky Russky Viestnik* is that adopted by James M. Evans, *Guide to the Amerikansky Russky Viestnik* (Fairview, N.J.: Carpatho-Rusyn Research Center, 1979).

37. *S. viek*, no. 78 (31 Mar. 1904), pp. 170–71.

38. *S. viek*, no. 82 (31 May 1904), pp. 307–9.

39. *S. viek*, no. 82 (31 May 1904), pp. 307–9.

40. At this time Warsaw was a part of the Russian Empire and no doubt the Slavic society there was dominated by Russians. *S. viek*, no. 64 (1 May 1903), p. 503.

41. *S. viek*, no. 65 (15 May 1903), p. 528.

42. *S. viek*, no. 65 (15 May 1903), p. 527.

43. *S. viek*, no. 65 (15 May 1903), p. 527.

44. "Religiozyi protektorat' Rossii na blizhnem' vostokie," *s. Viek*, no. 67 (15 Sept. 1903), pp. 581–90. The foregoing is a paraphrase, not a direct translation of the argument.

45. Russkii Skif', "Kto vinoven' v' makedonskoi rieznie?" [Who is the Culprit in the Macedonian Slaughter?], *S. viek*, no. 69 (15 Oct. 1903), pp. 642–45, specific quotation from p. 643.

46. Vergun, "Pan-Slavism or the Great Slavic Idea," *S. viek*, no. 82 (31 May 1904), pp. 290–95.

47. S. P. B., as cited in Vergun, "Pan-Slavism or the Great Slavic Idea," *S. viek*, no. 82.

48. S. P. B., as cited in Vergun, "Pan-Slavism or the Great Slavic Idea," *S. viek*, no. 82.

49. Vergun, "The Pan-Idea," *S. viek*, no. 65 (15 May 1903), pp. 514–17.

50. Vergun, "Pan-izme," S. viek, no. 72 (10 Dec. 1903), pp. 742–48.

51. Vergun, "Pan-izme," S. viek, no. 72 (10 Dec. 1903), p. 748.

52. Vergun, "Pan-izme," S. viek, no. 72 (10 Dec. 1903), p. 748; and Vergun, "German Seizure and Claims on Slavic Lands in the Near East," (Eastern Europe) S. viek (Nov.–Dec., 1904), Appendix to issues 88, 90, and 91–92 with continuous separate page numbers from 1–64.

53. Vergun, "Pan-izme"; and Vergun, "German Seizure and Claims on Slavic Lands in the Near East."

54. From an article by Bjornstjerne Bjornson, "How will Europe's Future for Next One-Hundred Years Be Determined?" was quoted in Trygve Tonstad, Bjornstjerne Bjornson og Slovakene (Oslo: Gyldendal Norsk Forlog, 1938), pp. 204–6 (in Norwegian, translated for me by Carl Chrislock).

55. Bjornstjerne Bjornson, "How will Europe's Future for Next One-Hundred Years Be Determined?"

56. This chapter contains only a summary description of this organization, but the society certainly deserves fuller treatment in a separate study.

57. S. viek, no. 62 (15 Feb. 1903), pp. 432–35.

58. S. viek, no. 62 (15 Feb. 1903), pp. 434–35, my paraphrase of original Russian.

59. S. viek, no. 62 (15 Feb. 1903), pp. 434–35.

60. "Slavians'kiia obshchestva," S. viek, no. 64 (1 May 1903), p. 501.

61. Tserkovnyi viestnik (St. Petersburg: St. Petersburg Theological Academy). These observations were based on an informal survey of the news weekly from the mid-1890s to 1915.

62. Tserkovnyi viestnik. These observations would reenforce the suggestion that Konstantin Podedonostsev was the architect of the Russian church's Galician policy. Pobedonostsev resigned as "over procurator" of the Holy Synod (governing body of the Russian church) in 1905 because he objected to constitutional government. Apparently, the church then left the more political forms of "cultural imperialism" to the secular societies such as the Galician-Russian Benevolent Society.

63. Criticism of Ruthenische Revue because it was published in German may not have been honest. Paul Magocsi indicates the journal was published in Vienna and its "purpose was to inform the Austrian public about contemporary conditions in the province [of Galicia]." See: Magocsi, Galicia (1983), p. 22.

64. "Galitsko-russkoe Blagotvoritel'noe Obshchestvo v S. Peterburgie," S. viek, no. 65 (15 May 1903), pp. 530–31.

65. "V Galitsko-russkom bratst'vie," S. viek, no. 72 (10 Dec. 1903), pp. 755–65.

66. "V Galitsko-russkom bratst'vie," S. viek, no. 72 (10 Dec. 1903), pp. 755–56.

67. "Slavians'kiia obshchestva," S. viek, no. 73 (10 Jan. 1904), pp. 21–22.

68. Otchet o dejatel'nosti Galitsko-russkago Blagotvoritel'nago Obshchestvo, pp. 13–14.

69. Otchet o dejatel'nosti Galitsko-russkago Blagotvoritel'nago Obshchestvo, pp. 13–14.

70. Otchet o dejatel'nosti Galitsko-russkago Blagotvoritel'nago Obshchestvo, pp. 9–10.

71. Otchet o dejatel'nosti Galitsko-russkago Blagotvoritel'nago Obshchestvo, pp. 9–10.

72. Otchet o dejatel'nosti Galitsko-russkago Blagotvoritel'nago Obshchestvo, p. 11

73. The above figures are from *Otchet o dejatel'nosti Galitsko-russkago Blagotvoritel'nago Obshchestvo*, pp. 42–43.
74. Zeman, *The Break-up of the Habsburg Empire*, pp. 3, 7–12.
75. Zeman, *The Break-up of the Habsburg Empire*, pp. 10–11.
76. This identification was given in each of the three pamphlets Denasii wrote in 1912 and 1913. Denasii, *Obrashchenie i prisoedienie na Athone avstriis'kago galichanina uniata v pravoslavie* (The Conversion and Return to Orthodoxy of a Galician Uniate on Mt. Athos) (Shamordino, 1913), *Athonskaja ikona presviatyia bogoroditsy* (The Athos Icon of our Holy Virgin) (Shamordino, 1913), and *Okruzhnoe poslanie s' Athona k' pravoslavnim khristianam'* (A Circular Letter from Athos to the Orthodox Christians) (Odessa, 1912).
77. Denasii, *A Circular Letter.*
78. Denasii, *The Athos Icon of Our Holy Virgin.*
79. Denasii, *The Conversion and Return to Orthodoxy.*
80. Zeman, *The Break-up of the Habsburg Empire*, p. 6.
81. Bishop Nicholas, "On the Duty Incumbent Not Alone on the Orthodox Russians But on the Orthodox of all Nationalities," *Russian-American Orthodox Messenger*, 1 Oct. 1894, pp. 34–40.
82. Zeman, *The Break-up of the Habsburg Empire*, pp. 7–8.
83. Zeman, *The Break-up of the Habsburg Empire*, pp. 8–9.
84. *Tserkovnyi viestnik*, no. 15 (1915): 453–55.
85. *Tserkovnyi viestnik*, no. 15 (1915): 453–55.
86. *Tserkovnyi viestnik*, no. 15 (1915): 453–55.

Chapter 3. The Influence of the Russian Orthodox Church on the Cultural Consciousness of the Rusyns in America

1. Bohdan P. Procko, "Pennsylvania: Focal Point of Ukrainian Immigration," in John E. Bodnar, *The Ethnic Experience in Pennsylvania* (Lewisburg, Pa.: Bucknell University Press, 1973), p. 218.
2. Many historians of immigration have made such observations. Walter Warzeski and Bohdan Procko have made that point with specific reference to the Rusyns. See: Walter C. Warzeski, "The Rusin Community in Pennsylvania," in Bodnar, *The Ethnic Experience*, p. 188; and Bohdan P. Procko, *Ukrainian Catholics in America* (Lanham, Md.: University Press of America, 1982), p. 2.
3. *Mesiatsoslov' Soedineniia* for 1912 (Munhall, Pa.: Greek Catholic Union Press, 1911), p. 161; and Introduction to, James M. Evans, *Guide to the Amerikansky Russky Viestnik Vol. I: 1894–1914* (Fairview, N.J.: Carpatho-Rusyn Research Center, 1979), p. 3. (Hereafter *Guide to the ARV.*)
4. *Mesiatsoslov' Soedinennia* for 1912, p. 162.
5. Luke Myshuha, "Ukrains'kyi Narodnyi Soiuz," in *Propamiatna knyha* (Jersey City, N.J.: Ukrainian National Union, 1936), pp. 195–96; and Introduction to *Guide to the ARV.*
6. Luke Myshuha, "Ukrains'kyi Narodnyi Soiuz," pp. 195–96; and Introduction to *Guide to the ARV.*
7. Luke Myshuha, "Ukrains'kyi Narodnyi Soiuz," pp. 195–96; and Introduction to *Guide to the ARV.*
8. Peter Kohanik, "Nachalo istorii amerikanskoi rusi," in Peter S. Hardy, ed., *Prikarpatskaja rus'* (Trumbull, Conn.: Peter S. Hardy, 1970), pp. 499–500.
9. Peter Kohanik, "Nachalo istorii amerikanskoi rusi," pp. 505–15.

10. Kohanik, "Nachalo istorii amerikanskoi rusi," p. 598.

11. Mikhail P. Baland "Do russkikh molodtsev," in *Kalendar dla 1911* (Philadelphia: Pravda, 1910), p. 74.

12. Baland, "Do russkikh molodtsev," p. 61.

13. "The Religious-national-cultural Movement of Ugro-Russian People in America," *Mesiatoslov' Soedineniia* for 1912, p. 64.

14. "The Religious-national-cultural Movement of Ugro-Russian People in America," p. 64.

15. "The Religious-national-cultural Movement of Ugro-Russian People in America," p. 166.

16. Procko, "Pennsylvania: Focal Point of the Ukrainian Immigration," p. 223.

17. *Tserkovnyi viestnik*, no. 7 (1896): 334ff.

18. "The Sting of the Russian Knout," *Svoboda*, 1 June 1899, p. 3.

19. Bishop Nicholas, "On the Duty Incumbent Not Alone on the Orthodox Russians But on the Orthodox of All Nationalities," *Russian Orthodox American Messenger*, 1 Oct. 1894, pp. 34–40.

20. Bishop Nicholas, "On the Duty Incumbent," pp. 36–39.

21. Hector Chevigny, *Russian America* (London: Cresset Press, 1965), pp. 65–70.

22. *Kalendar* for the Russian Orthodox church for 1950 (Wilkes Barre, Pa.: Svit, 1949), p. 209.

23. *Russian American Orthodox Messenger*, 1 Oct. 1896, pp. 34–40.

24. *Russian American Orthodox Messenger*, 1 Oct. 1896, pp. 34–40; and Dmitry Grigorieff, "The Orthodox Church in America from the Alaska Mission to Autocephaly," in *St. Vladimir's Theological Quarterly* 14, no. 4 (1970): 200.

25. Chevigny, *Russian America*, pp. 253–54.

26. Chevigny, *Russian America*, p. 262.

27. Grigorieff, *The Orthodox Church in America*, pp. 199–200.

28. Grigorieff, *The Orthodox Church in America*, p. 201.

29. *Kalendar*, 1950, p. 214.

30. Grigorieff, *The Orthodox Church in America*, p. 202.

31. This is the explanation offered by Dmitri Grigorieff in *The Orthodox Church in America*, p. 202.

32. Hector Chevigny describes this military dictatorship briefly in his chapter, "The Uprooting," *Russian America*, pp. 246–63.

33. The first time Toth's story was recorded was perhaps at the Wilkes Barre trials in 1894. This account has been quoted and discussed by Keith Rusin in "Father Alexis G. Toth and the Wilkes Barre Litigations," *St. Vladimir's Theological Quarterly* 16, no. 3 (1972): 128–49. Father Toth also recorded that account in several pamphlets published bilingually by the *Russian Orthodox American Messenger* and that account has since been quoted in numerous church anniversary albums and calendars. The following account is from the *75th Anniversary* Album of St. Mary's Russian Orthodox Greek Catholic Church (now called St. Mary's Orthodox Cathedral) in Minneapolis (Minneapolis, Minn.: St. Mary's, 1962), pp. 18–21.

34. Rusin, "Father Alexis G. Toth," pp. 128–30.

35. For a discussion on the Greek vs. the Latin rite in America, see discussion elsewhere in this work (chapter 5). For a recent biography of Archbishop John Ireland, see Marvin R. O'Connell, *John Ireland* (St. Paul: Minnesota Historical Society Press, 1988). This biography treats the incident between the Archbishop and Father Toth with some sympathy for Father Toth.

36. *The 75th Anniversary* album (St. Mary's in Minneapolis), p. 21.

37. Alex Simirenko, *Pilgrims, Colonists and Frontiersmen* (New York: Free Press of Glencoe, 1964).

38. *The 75th Anniversary* album,pp. 21–22.

39. *The 75th Anniversary* album, p. 23.

40. The story is recounted in Rusin, "Father Alexis G. Toth."

41. Keith Rusin (in "Father Alexis G. Toth") reported the following account as it was recorded in *The Wilkes-Barre Record*, 10 July 1893, p. 11.

42. *The Wilkes-Barre Record*, 10 July 1893, p. 11.

43. *Vsepoddaneishii otchet ober-prokurora Svjateshago Sinoda*, 1892–93, p. 413. (This publication was an annual report of the Holy Synod published in St. Petersburg, Russia.)

44. *Otchet ober-prokurora*, 1894–95, pp. 284–85.

45. *Otchet ober-prokurora*, 1896–97, pp. 160ff.

46. *Otchet ober-prokurora*, 1899, pp. 151–56.

47. *Otchet ober-prokurora*, 1899, pp. 151–56.

48. *Otchet ober-prokurora*, 1899, pp. 151–56.

49. *Otchet ober-prokurora*, 1900, pp. 267–72.

50. *Otchet ober-prokurora*, 1900, pp. 267–72.

51. Chevigny, *Russian America 1741–1867*.

52. *Otchet Pravoslavnavo Missionerskavo Obshchestva* (Moscow, 1903, pp. 2–3. (This publication was an annual report of the Orthodox Missionary Society.)

53. *Otchet Pravoslavnavo Missionerskavo Obshchestva*, 1903, pp. 2–3.

54. *Otchet Pravoslavnavo Missionerskavo Obshchestva*, 1903, pp. 49–54.

55. *Otchet Pravoslavnavo Missionerskavo Obshchestva*, 1903, pp. 2–3.

56. *Otchet ober-prokurora*, 1901, pp. 210–16.

57. *Otchet ober-prokurora* 1908–9, pp. 417–25.

58. Peter Kohanik, ed., *Russkoe pravoslavnoe Kafol. Obshchestvo Vzaimopomoshchi, 1895–1915* (New York, 1915), p. 23.

59. The three objectives were described in Kohanik, ed., *Russkoe Pravoslavnoe Kafol*, p. 13.

60. Kohanik, ed., *Russkoe Pravoslavnoe Kafol*, p. 13.

61. These observations are based on my analysis of these publications.

62. "A Brief History of the Russian Greek Orthodox Catholic Parish of Mayfield, Pa.," *Svit* (1 Feb. 1972), p. 1.

63. *Kalendar na god' 1950*, p. 218.

64. *Kalendar na god' 1950*, p. 216.

65. *Kalendar na god' 1950*, p. 217.

66. *Kalendar na god' 1950*, p. 218.

67. *Russian-American Orthodox Messenger* 4, no. 10 (28 May 1900).

68. Peter Kohanik, *The Austro-German Hypocrisy and the Russian Orthodox Greek Catholic Church* (New York, 1915), p. 9.

69. V. Markus pointed this out in the *Ukrainian Encyclopaedia:*

> This movement was financed by the Tsarist government and the Holy Synod in St. Petersburg. The objectives were political as well as proselytizing; to Russify the immigrants from the Austrian part of Ukraine and thus neutralize the increasingly anti-Russian attitudes in the homeland and of the immigrants.

V. Markus, "In the United States," in *Ukraine: A Concise Encyclopaedia*, vol. 2 (Toronto: University of Toronto Press, 1971), p. 1109.

70. Wasyl Halich also wrote that: "The Czarist regime sent to America hundreds of agents, or recruited them here, for the purpose of proselytizing the Ukrainian people, i.e., trying on American soil to convert them to Russian Orthodox religion and make Russians of them. To this end the government spent $77,850 annually." Wasyl Halich, *Ukrainians in the United States* (Chicago: University of Chicago Press, 1937), p. 103.

71. Iuliian Bachyns'kyi, *Ukrains'ka immigratsiia v Z'iedynenykh Derzhavakh Ameryky* (Ukrainian Immigrants in the United States of America) (Lviv: p.a., 1914), pp. 279–80. This observation may not be entirely correct when projected beyond this time period but for 1914, it probably is correct.

72. *Kalendar na god' 1950*, p. 219.

73. See discussion in Procko, *Ukrainian Catholics*, p. 15 and accompanying endnote.

74. Procko, *Ukrainian Catholics*, pp. 217–18.

75. John P. Dzubay, *Orthodoxy in America* (pamphlet) (Minneapolis, Minn., ca. 1955), no page numbers.

76. Dzubay, *Orthodoxy in America*.

77. "Twentieth Anniversary of the Demise of Metropolitan Macarius (Ilynsky)," *One Church* 27, no. 6 (1973): 277–80.

78. See "Necrolog" in *The Orthodox Church* 9, no. 4 (Apr. 1973): 6.

79. See "Nekrolog" in *Pravda* 67, no. 8 (Aug. 1969): 2.

80. Kohanik, "Nachalo istorii amerikanskoi rusi."

81. Regardless of the various possible meanings of the Cyrillic spelling, the union's official seal was subtitled in English as the "Russian National Union."

82. Kohanik, "Nachalo istorii amerikanskoi rusi," pp. 510–14.

83. M.L. 1908–XXIII/C-4102 (reel 18), pp. 3–5. See chapter 4, note 2 for an explanation of this citation.

84. Peter Kohanik, *70th Anniversary Russkoe Pravoslavnoe Obshchestvo Vzaimo-pomoshchi* (Wilkest Barre, Pa.: Svit, 1965), p. 29 and pp. 32–34.

85. Kohanik, *Russkoe Pravosloavnoe Kafto*, pp. 25–26.

86. Kohanik, *Russkoe Pravoslavnoe Kafto*, p. 76.

87. Kohanik, *Russkoe Pravoslavnoe Kafto*, p. 50.

88. Benedict Turkevich, *Pravoslavnoe Obschestvo Vzimopomoshch; 1896–1905* (Bridgeport, Conn., 1905), pp. 1, 5–7.

89. *Svit* (31 Aug. 1911), p. 5.

90. *Svit* (31 Aug. 1911), p. 5.

91. Balch, *Our Slavic Fellow Citizens*, p. 134.

92. "New Russian Reading Room," *Svit* 15 (23 July 1911), p. 2.

93. "From our Lives," *Svit* 15 (26 January 1911), p. 1.

94. "Iz chital'ni Miniapolisi," *Svit* 15 (2 Feb. 1911), p. 8.

95. *Svit* 75 (1 Feb. 1972), p. 1.

96. "Preosviashchenago Tikhona, arkhiepiskopa Aleutskago Sievero-Amerikanskago, ot' 24 Noiabria 1905 goda," in *Otzyvy po eparkhial'nykh arkhieveev' voprosu o tserkovnoi reformie*, pt. 1 (St. Petersburg, 1906), p. 534.

97. *Svit*, 15 (20 July 1911), p. 1.

98. *Svit* (13 Apr. 1911), p. 1, and no. 22 (15 June 1911), p. 1.

99. See *Russkii emigrant'* (26 Dec. 1912), p. 7 and (7 Mar. 1912), p. 3.

100. *Novii mir* (13 Aug. 1914), p. 5.

101. *Svit* (9 Feb. 1911), p. 3.

102. *Novii mir* (14 Mar. 1914), p. 3.

103. *Svit* (25 Jan. 1912), p. 2.

104. *Svit* (12 June 1912), p. 3.

105. *Svit* (27 June 1912), p. 3.
106. *Svit* (20 June 1912), p. 4 (headlines on p. 1).
107. *Svit* (20 June 1912), p. 3.
108. *Russkii emigrant'* (10 Oct. 1912), p. 7.
109. See biographical sketch in *Who Was Whom*, vol. 1 (Chicago: Marquis-Who's Who, 1963).
110. *Kalendar* for 1950 (Wilkes Barre, Pa.: Svit, 1949), pp. 116–17.
111. Tikhon, *Otzyvy*, pp. 534–37.
112. Tikhon, *Otzyvy*, pp. 530–31.
113. Tikhon, *Otzyvy*, 530–31.
114. *Kalendar* for 1910 (Svit), p. 56.
115. Tikhon, *Otzyvy*, pp. 530–31.
116. A. G. Toth, "How we Should Live in America," (in Slovak), pp. 129–31 in *Národný Kalendár* (Pittsburgh, Pa., 1899), also found in English translation by Mark Stolarik in *Makers of America*, vol. 5, *Natives and Aliens 1891–1903* (Chicago: Encyclopedia Britannica Educational Corp., 1971), pp. 242–45.
117. Toth, "How we Should Live in America."
118. That sentence was a subheadline in *The New York Times* (16 March 1913), Magazine section no. 6, p. 14.

Chapter 4. Hungarian Cultural and Nationalistic Activity within the Greek Catholic Church in America, 1900–1907

1. Much of the correspondence cited in this and the subsequent chapter are directed to the prime minister. No doubt it was directed to the office of the prime minister of Hungary. Some of the later correspondence is specifically directed to Alexander Wekerle who was a three-time prime minister of Hungary. During this period he was prime minister from 1906–10. See Robert A. Kahn, *A History of the Habsburg Empire, 1526–1918* (Berkeley: University of California Press, 1974), p. 456.

2. I have used microfilmed copies of materials from the Hungarian Foreign Ministers Archives *Miniszterelnoksegi Laveltar* (Magyar Orszagos Leveltar) hereafter identified as M.L.

Some years ago, the Immigration History Research Center (IHRC) selected material from the Hungarian archives relating to immigrants from Hungary to America and had them microfilmed. Copies of those microfilms are available at the Immigration History Research Center at the University of Minnesota. The documentary citations in this chapter will be followed by a reel number that will refer to the microfilm reel on which the documents are located.

Some of the documents were written in German, most in Magyar, and a few in English. The Magyar documents were translated in summary form by Maria Schweikert.

M.L. 1902-XXIII-852 (reel 1), pp. 10–22.

3. M.L. 1902-XXIII-852 (reel 1), pp. 10, 20–22.
4. M.L. 1902-XXIII-852 (reel 1), pp. 35–39.
5. M.L. 1902-XXIII-852 (reel 1), pp. 35–39.
6. M.L. 1902-XXIII-852 (reel 1), pp. 60–80 contains a copy of the indictment.
7. M.L. 1902-XXIII-852 (reel 1), pp. 25–26, unsigned and undated but early 1902; probably prepared by the minister of religion.

8. M.L. 1902-XXIII-852 (reel 1), pp. 25–26.
9. M.L. 1902-XXIII-852 (reel 1), pp. 25–26.
10. M.L. 1903-XVI-71 (reel 1), pp. 53–59.
11. M.L. 1903-XVI-71 (reel 1), pp. 53–59.
12. M.L. 1903-XX-834 (reel 3), pp. 54–56.
13. M.L. 1903-XX-834 (reel 3), pp. 54–56.
14. M.L. 1903-XX-834 (reel 3), pp. 93–99.
15. M.L. 1903-XX-834 (reel 3), pp. 93–99.
16. *NYT* (27 July 1903), p. 7, col. 3.
17. *NYT* (27 July 1903), p. 7, col. 3.
18. M.L. 1905-XX-1619 (reel 6), p. 38.
19. M.L. 1905-XX-1619 (reel 6), pp. 42–45.
20. Maria Mayer, "Zakarpatski Ukraintsi na perelomi stolit'," (Zacarpathian Ukrainians at the Turn of the Century) in *Zhovten' i ukrainska kultura* (Preshov: KSUT, 1968), pp. 68–69.
21. Maria Mayer, "Zakarpatski Ukraintsi," pp. 68–69; and M.L. 1905-XV-4632 (reel 4).
22. M.L. 1902-XXIII-852 (reel 1), pp. 25–26.
23. M.L. 1902-XXIII-852 (reel 1), pp. 25–26.
24. M.L. 1902-XXIII-852 (reel 1), pp. 25–26.
25. A good example of this correspondence is a letter dated 6 October 1904, where Hodobay reports on local efforts to select a bishop that would be contrary to Hungarian interests. M.L. 1906-XXI-854 (reel 10), p. 1322.
26. Warzeski, *Byzantine Rite Rusins*, pp. 95, 111–14.
27. M.L. 1902-XXIII-852 (reel 1), pp. 25–26.
28. M.L. 1906-XXI-854 (reel 10), pp. 1263–65.
29. M.L. 1906-XV-945 (reel 6), p. 150.
30. M.L. 1906-XXI-854 (reel 10), pp. 1263–65.
31. M.L. 1906-XXI-854 (reel 10), pp. 1263–65, and (reel 11), p. 2059.
32. Paul Magocsi, "The Political Activity of Rusyn-American Immigrants in 1918," *East European Quarterly* 10, no. 2 (1976): 347–65.
33. M.L. 1910-XXIII/B-2056 (reel 42), p. 422.
34. M.L. 1906-XXI-854 (reel 11), pp. 2366–68.
35. M.L. 1908-XXIII/C-4102 (reel 18), p. 100.
36. M.L. 1908-XXIII/C-4102 (reel 18), p. 129.
37. M.L. 1908-XXIII/C-4102 (reel 18), p. 251.
38. M.L. 1910-XXIII/B-2056 (reel 42), pp. 763–66.
39. M.L. 1910-XXIII/B-2056 (reel 42), pp. 252–53.
40. M.L. 1910-XXIII/B-2056 (reel 42), p. 254.
41. M.L. 1910-XXIII/B-2056 (reel 42), pp. 257–59.
42. M.L. 1910-XXIII/B-2056 (reel 42), pp. 260–61.
43. M.L. 1910-XXIII/B-2056 (reel 42), pp. 262–64.
44. M.L. 1910-XXIII/B-2056 (reel 42), pp. 265–68.
45. M.L. 1910-XXIII/B-2056 (reel 42), p. 302.
46. M.L. 1910-XXIII/B-2056 (reel 42), p. 301.
47. M.L. 1910-XXIII/B-2056 (reel 42), p. 469.
48. M.L. 1910-XXIII/B-2056 (reel 42), p. 287.
49. M.L. 1910-XXIII/B-2056 (reel 42), pp. 342–47.
50. M.L. 1910-XXIII/B-2056 (reel 42), p. 330.
51. M.L. 1910-XXIII-279 (reel 43), p. 621.
52. Warzeski, *Byzantine Rite Rusins*, p. 110.
53. M.L. 1906-XXI-854 (reel 10), p. 1322.

54. M.L. 1906-XXI-854 (reel 10), p. 1322.
55. M.L. 1906-XXI-854 (reel 11), p. 2066.
56. M.L. 1906-XXI-854 (reel 11), p. 2067.
57. M.L. 1906-XXI-854 (reel 11), pp. 2072–78.
58. M.L. 1906-XXI-854 (reel 11), pp. 2072–78.
59. M.L. 1906-XXI-854 (reel 11), p. 2351.
60. M.L. 1906-XXI-854 (reel 11), p. 2351.
61. M.L. 1906-XXI-854 (reel 11), pp. 2366–68.
62. M.L. 1907-XXIII/A-818 (reel 13), p. 487.
63. M.L. 1906-XXI-854 (reel 11), pp. 2328–31.
64. M.L. 1906-XXI-854 (reel 11), p. 2335.
65. M.L. 1906-XXI-854 (reel 11), pp. 2328–31.
66. M.L. 1906-XXI-854 (reel 1p. 2385–87.
67. M.L. 1906-XXI-854 (reel 11), pp. 2385–87.
68. M.L. 1906-XXI-854 (reel 11), p. 2388.
69. M.L. 1906-XXI-854 (reel 13), p. 2532.
70. M.L. 1907-XXIII/A-818 (reel 13), p. 48.
71. M.L. 1907-XXIII/A-818 (reel 13), p. 52.
72. M.L. 1907-XXIII/A-818 (reel 18), pp. 53–54.
73. M.L. 1907-XXIII/A-818 (reel 13), pp. 55–56.
74. I do not know who the choice of the American priests was. Warzeski in *Byzantine Rite Rusins* (p. 114) mentions the congress and draws his information about it from *Amerikansky Russky Viestnik* but he does not indicate who the choice was and neither does the correspondence in the ML. If they had agreed on a nominee, it would probably have been Rev. Dzubay, who was the recognized elder of the Greek Catholic priests and a very capable administrator who had helped found numerous congregations.
75. M.L. 1907-XXIII/A-818 (reel 13), pp. 55–56.
76. M.L. 1907-XXIII/A-818 (reel 13), pp. 57–58.
77. M.L. 1907-XXIII/A-818 (reel 13), p. 65.

Chapter 5. Conflicts in the Establishment of the Greek Catholic Church in America

1. Walter Warzeski suggested, "perhaps the greatest number left because of the neglect and hostility of the Latin Rite." *Byzantine Rite Rusins*, pp. 104–5.
2. Procko, *Ukrainian Catholics*, p. 16.
3. O'Connell, *John Ireland*, p. 270.
4. Gerald P. Fogarty, S. J., "The American Hierarchy and Oriental Rite Catholics, 1890–1907," in *Records of the American Catholic Historical Society of Philadelphia* 85 (Mar.–June 1974), p. 18.
5. Msgr. Basil Shereghy, ed., *A Historical Album*, (McKeesport, Pa.: United Societies of the U.S.A., 1978), p. 25.
6. See "Ministerial Communication no. 393," M.L. 1903-XX-834 (reel 3), pp. 54–56.
7. Procko, *Ukrainian Catholics*, p. 12 and elsewhere; and Warzeski, *Byzantine Rite Rusins*, p. 114ff. and elsewhere.
8. Procko, pp. 14ff. and Warzeski, pp. 112–28.
9. Quoted in Fogarty, "The American Hierarchy," p. 20.
10. Examples will follow in this chapter.

11. See discussion in earlier chapter..

12. Procko, *Ukrainian Catholics in America*, pp. 28–29.

13. According to official Hungarian statistics published in Budapest in 1902, there were a total of 262,815 GreekCatholic Rusyn immigrants to the United States from Galicia and Subcarpathia. Of these 262,815 people, 70 percent or 190,935 were from Subcarpathia, while only 30 percent or 81,829 were from Galicia. (M.L. 1903-XVI-71 (reel 1), pp. 53–69. These percentages changed somewhat in the following years as immigration from Galicia increased. But the Russian Orthodox *Kalendar'* for 1910 (p. 56) indicated that of its 18,224 Rusyn members, 65 percent or 11,794 came from Galicia while 35 percent or 5,430 came from Subcarpathia. These figures indicate the 1907 situation (the 1910 *Kalendar'* was published in 1909 with 1908 statistics).

14. Warzeski, *Byzantine Rite Rusins*, p. 102.

15. Keith Rusin, "Father Alexis Toth and the Wilkes Barre Litigations," pp. 128–49.

16. See Father Alexis Toth story in chapter 3.

17. The story is retold in *St. Mary's Golden Jubilee Album* (Minneapolis: St. Mary's Russian Orthodox Greek Catholic Church, 1937).

18. M.L. 1902-XXIII-852 (reel 1), pp. 10–26.

19. Quoted by Vladimir C. Nahirny and Joshua Fishman in "Ukrainian Language Maintenance Efforts in The-United States," in Fishman, et al., *Language Loyalty in the United States* (The Hague: Mouton, 1966), p. 335.

20. Philip Gleason, *The Conservative Reformers: German-American Catholics and Social Order* (Notre Dame, Ind.: University of Notre Dame, 1968).

21. Colman J. Barry, *Catholic Church and German Americans* (Milwaukee, Wisc.: Bruce, 1953).

22. M.L. 1906-XXI-854 (reel 11), P. 2057.

23. M.L. 1906-XXI-854 (reel 11), p. 2058.

24. M.L. 1906-XXI-854 (reel 11), p. 2062.

25. M.L. 1906-XXI-854 (reel 11), p. 2059.

26. M.L. 1906-XXI-854 (reel 11), pp. 2062–63.

27. M.L. 1906-XXI-854 (reel 11), pp. 2062–63.

28. M.L. 1906-XXI-854 (reel 11), p. 2066.

29. M.L. 1906-XXI-854 (reel 11), p. 2066.

30. M.L. 1906-XXI-854 (reel 11), p. 2067.

31. M.L. 1906-XV-1737 (reel 6), p. 53.

32. M.L. 1906-XV-1737 (reel 6), p. 55.

33. M.L. 1907-XXIII-286 (reel 13), p. 6.

34. M.L. 1910-XXII/B-927 (reel 40), p. 2037.

35. M.L. 1910-XXII/B-927 (reel 40), p. 2183ff.

36. M.L. 1910-XXII/B-927 (reel 40), p. 2183ff.

37. M.L. 1906-XXI-854 (reel 11), pp. 2328–31.

38. M.L. 1907-XXIII/B-816 (reel 13), pp. 10–15.

39. M.L. 1907-XXIII/B-816 (reel 13), p. 19.

40. M.L. 1907-XXIII/B-816 (reel 13), p. 26.

41. M.L. 1907-XXIII/B-816 (reel 13), pp. 27–32.

42. M.L. 1907-XXIII/B-816 (reel 13), p. 33.

Warzeski, *Byzantine Rite Rusins*, pp. 110–11.

44. M.L. 1906-XXI-854 (reel 11), pp. 2328–31.

45. M.L. 1906-XXI-854 (reel 11), p. 2335.

46. This conflict was discussed on numerous occasions during the discussion over the appointment of a bishop. Mr. Hengelmuller, the Austrian ambas-

sador to Washington, mentioned this fact in a letter to the apostolic delegate suggesting that the divisions in the church "arise from national feelings and political agitations." M.L. 1906-XXI-854 (reel 11), pp. 2385–87.

47. M.L. 1906-XXI-854 (reel 11), pp. 2456-57.

48. M.L. 1906-XXI-854 (reel 11), pp. 2328–31.

49. M.L. 1906-XXI-854 (reel 11), p. 2509.

50. Warzeski, *Byzantine Rate Rusins*, p. 202.

51. M.L. 1910-XXII/B-927 (reel 40), p. 2182.

52. M.L. 1910-XXII/B-927 (reel 40), p. 2036.

53. M.L. 1906-XXI-854 (reel 11), p. 2454.

54. Warzeski, *Byzantine Rite Rusins*, p. 202.

55. Warzeski, *Byzantine Rite Rusins*, p. 203.

56. Rusin, "Father Alexis Toth."

57. Rusin, "Father Alexis Toth."

58. M.L. 1906-XXI-854 (reel 11), p. 2062.

59. M.L. 1906-XXI-854 (reel 11), p. 2063.

60. M.L. 1906-XV-1737 (reel 6), p. 55.

61. Warzeski, *Byzantine Rite Rusins*, p. 202.

62. Rusin, "Father Alexis Toth," pp. 140–42.

63. M.L. 1908-XXIII/C-4102 (reel 18), p. 100.

64. M.L. 1908-XXIII/C-4102 (reel 18), p. 100.

65. Warzeski, *Byzantine Rite Rusins*, p. 114.

66. M.L. 1906-XXI-854 (reel 11), pp. 2366–68.

67. M.L. 1906-XXI-854 (reel 11), pp. 2366–68.

68. Letter from Korotnoki to the Hungarian prime minister. M.L. 1908-XXIII/C-4102 (reel 18), p. 129.

69. The bishops' letters to the prime minister, M.L. 1908-XXIII/C-4102 (reel 18), pp. 170, 176.

70. A Letter to the Hungarian secretary of state from the consul in Philadelphia, M.L. 1908 1908-XXIII/C-4102 (reel 18), p. 251.

71. M.L. 1904-XVI-5089 (reel 3), pp. 9–10.

72. A letter from the foreign minister's office in Vienna to Dr. Wekerle, the prime minister of Hungary dated 1 Mar. 1907, M.L. 1907-XXIII/A-818 (reel 13), pp. 57–58.

73. Warzeski, *Byzantine Rite Rusins*, pp. 114–26.

74. Warzeski, *Byzantine Rite Rusins*, pp. 114–26; and M.L. 1907-XXIII/A-818 (reel 13), p. 478ff.

75. Warzeski, *Byzantine Rite Rusins*, pp. 114–26; and M.L. 1907-XXIII/A-818 (reel 13), p. 478ff.

76. M.L. 1907-XXIII/A-818 (reel 13), p. 478ff.

Epilogue: The Fruits of Propaganda and Rivalry

1. "To Seek Sympathy for Hungarian Liberty," *NYT* (5 July 1914), sec. 5, p. 10.

2. *NYT* (16 Mar. 1913), sec. 6, p. 14.

3. Alexander Konta was born in Budapest 11 May 1863, and emigrated to the United States in 1887. *Who Was Who in America*, vol. 1 (Chicago: Marquis-Who's Who, 1963).

4. *NYT* (16 Mar. 1913), sec. 6, p. 14.

5. *NYT* (31 May 1914), sec. 2, p. 4.

6. NYT (31 May 1914), sec. 2, p. 4.

7. NYT (5 July 1914), sec. 5, p. 10.

8. NYT (6 July 1914), p. 6.

9. NYT (6 July 1914), p. 6.

10. NYT (5 July 1914), sec. 3, p. 4.

11. NYT (6 Sept. 1914), p. 1.

12. NYT (27 May 1915), sec. 5, p. 10.

13. NYT (16 Sept. 1915), p. 2.

14. NYT (13 Oct. 1915), p. 16.

15. Ustav' severo-amerikanskago provoslavnago bratstva vo imia Sv. Rav-noapostol'nago Knjaza Vladimira v' Petrogradie (Petrograd, 1915).

16. NYT (5 Feb. 1915), p. 5.

17. The Russian Club of America (New York, 1915).

18. Wasyl Halich, "The Ukrainian Americans: Early Struggles, Personal and Institutional 1865–1938," manuscript in IHRC, pp. 8–9.

19. Peter Kohanik, The Austro-German Hypocrisy and the Russian Ortho-dox Greek Catholic Church (New York, 1915).

20. NYT (16 May 1913), sec. 6, p. 14.

21. Kohanik, The Austro-German Hypocrisy, pp. 18–19.

22. Kohanik, The Austro-German Hypocrisy, pp. 18–19.

23. Gustaff F. Steffen, Russia, Poland, and the Ukraine, trans. J. W. Hartmann (Jersey City, N.J.: Ukrainian National Council, 1915), p. 8; and Vladimir Stepankovsky, The Russian Plot to Seize Galicia (Jersey City, N.J.: Ukrainian National Council, 1915), p. 9.

24. Steffen, Russia, Poland, p. 8; and Stepankovsky, The Russian Plot, p. 9.

25. Stefan Rudnitsky, The Ukraine and the Ukrainians (Jersey City, N.J.: Ukrainians National Council, 1915).

26. Rudnitsky, The Ukraine, p. 36.

27. Victor S. Mamatey, "The Slovaks and Carpatho-Ruthenians," in Joseph P. O'Grady, ed., The Immigrants' Influence on Wilson's Peace Policies (Lexington: University of Kentucky Press, 1967), p. 249.

28. Paul Magocsi, "The Political Activity of Rusyn American Immigrants in 1918," East European Quarterly 10, no. 2 (1976): 347–65.

29. Magocsi, "The Political Activity of Rusyn American Immigrants"; also see a Ukrainian account in Derzhavni zmagannia Prykarpatskoi Ukrainy (no author) (Vienna, 1924), pp. 5–8; and Warzeski, Byzantine Rite Rusins. pp. 146–50.

Essay on Sources

The Introduction and Chapter 1 of this study provide an introduction to the cultural crisis in Galicia and Subcarpathia from 1848 to 1914. These chapters are based primarily on secondary sources. Some of these sources were published in the time period under discussion, however. For example, the biography of Mykhailo Kachkovs'kyi by Bogdan Dieditskii, ed., *Mikhail Kachkovskii: l sovremennaia galitsko-russkaia literatura* (Lvov [Lviv]: Stavropigian Institute, 1876); And the biographical sketch of Ioann Naumovich: *Pamiati Protoiereia Ioanna Grigorevicha Naumovicha* (Odessa: Galician-Russian Benevolent Society, 1912).

Chapter 2 surveys Russian activities among the Rusyns in Galicia and Subcarpathia. The material for this chapter came from pamphlets, journals, memoirs, and "Proceedings" of several Russian organizations in addition to some secondary sources. The most important sources were: The Pan-Slavic Journal, *Slavianskii viek*, edited by Dmitri Vergun and published in Vienna from 1901 to 1904. The reports of the Galician-Russian Benevolent Society, *Otchet o dieiatel'nosti Galitsko-russkago Blagotvoritel'nago Obshchestva* were published in St. Petersburg in the decade preceding the First World War. *Tserkovnyi viestnik*, published in St. Petersburg, was an official publication of the St. Petersburg Theological Academy.

These and numerous other materials were found in the St. Nicholas Collection. The St. Nicholas Collection is a major part of the archives of the Russian Orthodox mission in North America and was housed at the Immigration History Research Center (IHRC) at the University of Minnesota. The collection has now been rejoined with the rest of the archives of the American Orthodox church in Syosset, New York.

Another significant source for monographic materials is the Ukrainian Collection at the IHRC. That collection contains thousands of books, pamphlets, and *Kalendars* written from the Rusyn perspective as well as the Ukrainian viewpoint. Many of these works have been listed in a bibliography compiled by the collection's curator, Halyna Myroniuk, *Ukrainians in North America: A Select Bibliography* (St. Paul: Immigration History Research Center, University of Minnesota; Toronto: Multicultural History Society of Ontario, 1981).

The third chapter of this work examines some aspects of the activities of the Russian Orthodox mission among the Rusyns in the United States. This discussion is based primarily on the *Kalendars* of the various Russian-oriented fraternal societies such as the Russian Brotherhood Organization and the Russian Orthodox Mutual Aid Society. Because the Russian Orthodox Mutual Aid Society was a central organization for the Russian mission, its weekly newspaper, *Svit*, was also used extensively in this chapter. Many of these and similar works are available in the Russian and Carpatho-Russian collections of the IHRC.

While no index has been compiled for *Svit*, indexes have been compiled for two other newspapers that figure prominently in any discussion of Rusyns (or Ukrainians) in America: James M. Evans compiled a *Guide to the Amerikansky Russky Viestnik Volume I: 1894–1914* (Fairview, N.J.: Carpatho-Rusyn Research Center, 1979). The *Amerikansky Russky Viestnik* was the voice of the Greek Catholic Union, the largest society of Subcarpathian Rusyns. A guide to *Svoboda* has recently been compiled by Walter Anastas and Maria Woroby, *A Select Index To Svoboda, Volume One: 1893–1899* (St. Paul: Immigration History Research Center, University of Minnesota, 1990). *Svoboda* was the official publication of the Ruskyi Narodnyi Soiuz (now called the Ukrainian National Association).

The primary sources for official Russian interests in the American mission were the annual reports of the administrative officer of the Holy Synod, *Vsepoddanneishii otchet ober-prokurora Sviateishago Synoda*; and the annual reports of the Orthodox Missionary Society, *Otchet Pravoslavnago Missionerskago Obshchestva*. These two organizations were the official agencies responsible for the American mission. The Holy Synod was the supreme governing body of the Russian Orthodox church. The Orthodox Missionary Society was a semiofficial missionary society that was instructed by Tsar Nicholas to share in the responsibilities for the American mission in 1900.

Other Russian sources were the journals, *Tserkovnyi viestnik*, the official publication of the St. Petersburg Theological Academy and *Bogoslovskii viestnik*, the official publication of the Moscow Theological Academy.

Several of the early Orthodox missionaries wrote histories or left accounts worthy of consideration. Good examples of this type of information source are B. M. Bensin, *History of the Russian Greek Catholic Church of North America* (New York, 1941), and Peter Kohanik, *Nachalo istorii amerikanskoi rusi* (reprint Trumbull, Conn.: Peter S. Hardy, 1970).

Chapters 4 and 5 discuss the Hungarian government's interests in the Rusyns in the United States and the establishment of the Greek Catholic rite in America. The primary sources for these chapters are microfilms of materials from the Hungarian State Archives in Budapest, The Magyar Orszagos Leveltar. The Hungarian State Archives were searched for materials on the immigration of people from Hungary to the United

States. These materials were microfilmed in Hungary and are now available on sixty-five reels of microfilm at the IHRC.

The final chapter discusses activities affecting the Rusyn community during and after the First World War, and includes analyses of previously published works, eyewitness accounts, and accounts in *The New York Times*, which at times reflected the public response to events.

Bibliography

Bibliographical Guides

There are several significant bibliographical guides essential to any survey of Rusyn studies. Paul R. Magocsi has published several historical surveys and bibliographical guides to the American and the European areas of Rusyn studies. His works: *The Shaping of a National Identity: Subcarpathian Rus', 1848–1948* (Cambridge: Harvard University Press, 1978); and *Galicia: A Historical Survey and Bibliographic Guide* (Toronto, Buffalo, and London: University of Toronto Press, 1983) provide excellent narrative and bibliographical surveys of Subcarpathia and Galicia.

Magocsi also offers several similar surveys of the Rusyns in America. His *Carpatho-Ruthenians in North America*. The Balch Institute Historical Reading Lists, no. 31 (Philadelphia,1976) lists forty-three important works on Carpatho-Rusyns in Eastern Europe and in the United States. He contributed to a catalog of Carpatho-Rusyn holdings in the Harvard University Library in: Paul R. Magocsi and Olga K. Mayo, Compilers, *Carpatho-Ruthenica at Harvard: A Catalog of Holdings* (Englewood, N.J.: Transworld Publishers, 1977). Magocsi also compiled *The Peter Jacyk Collection of Ukrainian Serials: A Guide to Newspapers and Periodicals* (Toronto: University of Toronto Chair of Ukrainian Studies, 1983). This collection lists 175 newspapers and journals published in Subcarpathia from 1848 to 1918 that are on microfilm at the University of Toronto.

Paul R. Magocsi, *Our People: Carpatho-Rusyns and Their Descendants in North America* (Toronto: Multicultural History Society of Ontario, 1984; revised 1985) provides an excellent historical survey and a comprehensive bibliography of the Carpatho-Rusyns in North America.

And finally, Paul Robert Magocsi, *Carpatho-Rusyn Studies: An Annotated Bibliography, Volume I: 1975–1984* (New York and London: Garland Publishing, Inc., 1988) is an exhaustive annotated guide to virtually all works on Subcarpathians published between the years cited in the title. He expects to follow this volume with volume 2 covering the following decade.

There are several other bibliographies useful for the study of the Subcarpathians. Edward Kasinec, *The Carpatho-Ruthenian Immigration in the United States: A Note on Sources in Some United States Repositories*, Harvard Ukrainian Research Institute Offprint Series, no. 6 (Cambridge, 1975) provided a useful survey of some of the materials in a number of American libraries and archives. Frank Renkiewicz, *The Carpatho-Ruthenian Microfilm Project: A Guide to Newspapers and Periodicals* (St. Paul: Immigration History Research Center, University of Minnesota, 1979) lists sixty-two titles that were microfilmed as part of a microfilming project partially sponsored by the Byzantine Ruthenian Metropolitan Provence of Pittsburgh.

The newsletter, *Carpatho-Rusyn American* (published four times a year since

1978) (Fairview, N.J.: Carpatho-Rusyn Research Center) is another very important source for general information, book reviews, and literature surveys about Carpatho-Rusyns in America and Europe.

Select Bibliography

Bachyns'kyi, Iuliian. *Ukrains'ka immigratsiia v Z'iedynenykh Derzhavakh Ameryky* (Ukrainian Immigrants in the United States of America). Lviv: p.a., 1914.

Balch, Emily Green. *Our Slavic Fellow Citizens*. Reprint of 1910 edition. New York: Arno Press, 1969.

Baran, Alexander. "Carpatho-Ukrainian Emigration, 1870–1914." In *New Soil-Old Roots: The Ukrainian Experience in Canada*, edited by Jaroslav Rozumnyj, pp. 252–75. Winnipeg: Ukrainian Academy of Arts and Sciences in Canada, 1983.

Berry, Coleman J. *Catholic Church and German Americans*. Milwaukee, Wisc.: Bruce, 1953.

Bidwell, Charles E. *The Language of Carpatho-Ruthenian Publications in America*. Pittsburgh, Pa.: University Center For International Studies, University of Pittsburgh, 1971.

Bodnar, John E., ed. *The Ethnic Experience in Pennsylvania*. Lewisburg, Pa.: Bucknell University Press, 1973.

Boysak, Basil. *The Fate of the Holy Union in Carpatho-Ukraine*. Toronto and New York: n.p., 1963.

Byrnes, Robert F. *Pobedonostsev, his Life and Thought*. Bloomington: Indiana University Press, 1968.

Capek, Thomas. *Slavs in the United States Census, 1850–1940*. Chicago: The Czechoslovak National Council of America, 1943.

Chevigny, Hector. *Russian America*. London: Cresset Press, 1965.

Chubaty, Nicholas D. "Moscow and the Ukrainian Church after 1654." *The Ukrainian Quarterly* 9 no. 3 (1953): 60–70.

Davis, Jerome. *The Russians in America, Bolsheviks or Brothers?*. New York: George H. Doran, 1922.

————. *The Russian Immigrant*. New York: The Macmillan Co., 1922.

Dragan, A. *Ukrainian National Association: Its Past and Present, 1894–1964*. Jersey City, N.J.: Ukrainian National Association, 1964.

Duchnovic, Alexander. *The History of the Eparchy of Prjasev*. Translated by Athanasius B. Pekar. Rome: Published by JUH, 1971.

Dyrud, Keith P. "East Slavs: Rusins, Ukrainians, Russians and Belorussians." In *They Chose Minnesota: A Survey of the State's Ethnic Groups*, edited by June Drenning Holmquist, pp. 405–22. St. Paul: Minnesota Historical Society, 1981.

Dyrud, Keith P. and James W. Cunningham. *Heirs of Byzantium: Eastern Christianity in Minnesota*. Offprint, *Modern Greek Studies Yearbook* (Minneapolis, Minn., 1989).

Fogarty, Gerald P. "The American Hierarchy and Oriental Rite Catholics, 1890–

1907." *Records of the American Catholic Historical Society of Philadelphia* 85 (Mar.–June 1974): 17–21.

Frantsev, V. A. "Iz istorii bor'by za russkii literaturnyi iazyk' v' Podkarpatskoi Rusi v polovine XIX st." In *Karpatorusskii sbornik*, pp. 1–49. Uzhgorod, 1930.

Gleason, Philip. *The Conservative Reformers: German-American Catholics and Social Order.* Notre Dame, Ind.: University of Notre Dame, 1968.

Grigorieff, Dmitri. "The Orthodox Church in America from the Alaska Mission to Autocephaly." *St. Vladimir's Theological Quarterly* 14, no. 4 (1970): 196–218.

Gulovich, Stephen C. *Windows Westward Rome-Russia-Reunion.* New York: D. X. McMullen Co., 1947.

———. "The Rusin Exarchate in the United States." *Eastern Churches Quarterly* 6 (1946): 459–85.

Halecki, Oscar. *From Florence to Brest: 1439–1596.* New York: Fordham University Press, 1958.

Halich, Wasyl. *Ukrainians in the United States.* Chicago: University of Chicago Press, 1937.

———. "The Ukrainian Americans: Early Struggles, Personal and Institutional (1865–1918)." Manuscript in Immigration History Research Center, University of Minnesota, St. Paul, Minn.

Himka, John-Paul. "Priests and Peasants: The Greek Catholic Pastor and the Ukrainian National Movement in Austria, 1867–1900." *Canadian Slavonic Papers* 21, no. 1 (Offprint, 1986): 1–14.

———. *Socialism in Galicia.* Cambridge: Harvard University Press, 1983.

———. "The Greek Catholic Church and Nation-Building, 1772–1918", *Harvard Ukrainian Studies* (Cambridge: Harvard Ukrainian Research Institute) 8, no. 3/4 (Offprint, 1986): 426–52.

———. "The Ukrainian National Movement before 1914." In *Morality and Reality: The Life and times of Andrei Sheptyts'kyi*, edited by Paul Robert Magocsi, pp. 31–46. Edmonton, Alberta: Canadian Institute of Ukrainian Studies, 1989.

Jurchisin, Mitro, comp. *Carpathian Village People: A Listing of Immigrants to Minneapolis, Minnesota from the 1880s to 1947.* Minneapolis, Minn.: By Author, 1981.

Kann, Robert A. *The Multinational Empire: Nationalism and National Reform in the Habsburg Monarchy.* 2 vols. New York: Columbia University Press, 1950.

———. *A History of the Habsburg Empire 1526–1918.* Berkeley: University of California Press, 1974.

Kann, Robert A. and David V. Zdenek. *The Peoples of the Eastern Habsburg Lands, 1526–1918.* Seattle: University of Washington Press, 1984.

Kimball, Stanley B. *The Austro-Slav Revival: A Study of Nineteenth Century Literary Foundations.* Philadelphia: The American Philosophical Society, 1973.

Kohanik, Peter. *70th Anniversary Russkoe Pravoslavnoe Obshchestvo Vziamopomoshchi.* Wilkes Barre, Pa.: Svit, 1965.

———. The Austro-German Hypocrisy and the Russian Orthodox Greek Catholic Church. New York, 1915.

———. Nachalo istorii amerikanskoi rusi. Reprinted in Peter S. Hardy, ed. Prikarpatskaja Rus'. Trumbull, Conn.: Published by Peter S. Hardy, 1970.

———, ed. Russkoe Pravoslavnoe Kafol. Obshchestvo Vzaimopomoshchi, 1895–1915. New York: 1915.

Kohn, Hans. Pan Slavism, Its History and Ideology. Notre Dame, Ind.: Notre Dame University Press, 1953.

Kozik, Jan. Ukrainian National Movement in Galicia: 1815–1849. Edmonton, Alberta: Canadian Institute of Ukrainian Studies, 1986.

Kubijovyc, Volodymyr, ed. Encyclopedia of Ukraine. Toronto, Buffalo, and London: University of Toronto Press, 1984–.

———, ed. The Ukraine: A Concise Encyclopaedia. 2 vols. Toronto: Ukrainian National Association by the University of Toronto Press, 1963–71.

Kuropas, Myron. The Ukrainians in America. Minneapolis, Minn.: Lerner Press, 1972.

Lacko, Michael. The Union of Uzhorod. Cleveland, Ohio: Slovak Institute, 1976.

Macartney, C. A. Hungary and Her Successors. London and New York: Oxford University Press, 1937.

———. The Habsburg Empire, 1790–1918. New York: Macmillan, 1969.

Magocsi, Paul Robert. Carpatho-Rusyn Studies: An Annotated Bibliography Volume I: 1975–1984. New York: Garland Publishing, Inc., 1988.

———. Galicia: A Historical Survey and Bibliographic Guide. Toronto: University of Toronto Press, 1983.

———. "The Political Activity of Rusyn-American Immigrants in 1918." East European Quarterly (Boulder, Colo.) 10, no. 3 (1976): 347–65.

———. The Rusyn Ukrainians of Czechoslovakia: An Historical Survey. Bausteine zur ethnopolitichen Forschung, vol. 7. Vienna: Wilhelm Braumuller Universitatis-Verlagsbuchhandlung, 1983.

———. Our People: Carpatho-Rusyns and Their Descendants in North America. Toronto: Multicultural History Society of Ontario, 1984.

———. The Shaping of a National Identity: Subcarpathian Rus', 1848–1948. Cambridge: Harvard University Press, 1978.

Mamatey, Victor S. The United States and East Central Europe, 1914–1918. Princeton: Princeton University Press, 1957.

———. "The Slovaks and Carpatho-Ruthenians." In The Immigrants' Influence on Wilson's Peace Policies, edited by Joseph P. O'Grady, pp. 224–49. Lexington: University of Kentucky Press, 1976.

Markus, Vasil. "An Examination of the Problem of Examining the History of the Ukrainian Immigrant in America." The Ukrainian Historian 8, nos. 1–2 (1971): 70–80.

Mayer, Maria. "Some Aspects of the Development of the National Movement amongst the Ruthenes of Hungary (Sub-Carpathian Ruthenia) 1849–1914." In Studies in East European Social History, vol. 1, edited by Keith Hitchens, pp. 177–91. Leiden: E. J. Brill, 1977.

────. "Zakarpats'ki Ukraintsi na perelomi stolit." *Zhovten' i ukrains'ka kul'tura*, pp. 49–73. Prešov: KSUT, 1968.

Myshuha, Luka. "Ukrains'kyi Narodnyi Soiuz." In *Propamiatna knyha*, pp. 193–207. Jersey City, N.J.: Ukrainian National Association, 1936.

Nahirny, Vladimir C. and Joshua Fishman. "Ukrainian Language Maintenance Efforts in the United States." In *Language Loyalty in the United States*, edited by Joshua Fishman. The Hague: Mouton, 1966.

O'Connell, Marvin R. *John Ireland and the American Catholic Church*. St. Paul: Minnesota Historical Society Press, 1988.

Otzyvy eparkhial'nykh arkhiereev po voprosu o tserkovnoi reforme. 3 vols. St. Petersburg: Sinodal'naia Tipografiia, 1906.

Panas, I. O. "Karpatorusskie otzvuki russkago pokhoda v Vengrii 1849 goda." In *Karpatorusskii sbornik*. Uzhgorod: Subcarpathian Enlightenment Union, 1930.

Pekar, Athanasius. *Historic Background of the Eparchy of Prjashev*. Pittsburgh, Pa.: Byzantine Seminary Press, 1968.

────. "Historical Background of the Carpatho-Ruthanians in America." *Ukrajins'kyi istoryk* (New York, Toronto, and Munich) 13, nos. 1–4 (1976): 87–102 and 14, nos. 1–2 (1977): 70–84.

Petrovich, Michael B. *The Emergence of Russian Pan-Slavism, 1856–1870*. New York: Columbia University Press, 1956.

Procko, Bohdan. "Sotor Ortynsky: First Ruthenian Bishop in the United States, 1907–1916." *Catholic Historical Review* 58, no. 4 (1973): 513–33.

────. *Ukrainian Catholics in America*. Lanham, Md.: University Press of America, 1982.

────. "The Establishment of the Ruthenian Church in the United States, 1884–1907." *Pennsylvania History* (Bloomsburg, Pa.) 42, no. 2 (1975): 137–54.

Pysh, Simeon. *A Short History of Carpatho-Russia*. Translated by A. J. Yurkovsky. Trumbull, Conn.: s.n., 1973.

Renoff, Richard. "Carpatho-Ruthenian Resources and Assimilation, 1880–1924: A Preliminary Survey." *Review Journal of Philosophy and Social Science* (Meerut City, India) 2, no. 1 (1977): 53–78.

Rudnitsky, Stefen. *The Ukraine and the Ukrainians*. Jersey City, N.J.: Ukrainian National Council, 1915.

Rudnytsky, Ivan L. "Ukrainians in Galicia under Austrian Rule." *Austrian History Yearbook* 3, no. 2 (1967): 394–429.

Rusin, Keith. "Father Alexis G. Toth and the Wilkes Barre Litigations." *St. Vladimir's Theological Quarterly* 16, no. 3 (1972): 128–49.

Scotus, Viator (R. W. Seton-Watson). *Racial Problems in Hungary*. London: A. Constable & Co., 1908.

Senyshyn, Ambrose. "The Ukrainian Catholics in the United States." *Eastern Churches Quarterly* 6 (Oct.–Dec. 1946): 439–53.

Shereghy, Basil. *The Byzantine Catholics*. Pittsburgh, Pa.: Byzantine Seminary Press, 1981.

────, ed. *The United Societies of the U.S.A.: A Historical Album*. McKeesport, Pa.: The United Societies, 1978.

Simirenko, Alex. *Pilgrims, Colonists and Frontiersmen*. New York: Free Press of Glencoe, 1964.

Slivka, John, comp. *Historical Mirror: Sources of the Rusin and Hungarian Greek Rite Catholic in the United States of America, 1884–1963*. Brooklyn, N.Y.: By John Slivka, 1978.

Stavrou, Theofanis. *Russian Interests in Palestine, 1882–1914*. Thessaloniki: Institute for Balkan Studies, 1963.

Steffen, Gustaff F. *Russia, Poland, and the Ukraine*. Translated by J. W. Hartman. Jersey City, N.J.: Ukrainian National Council, 1915.

Stepankovsky, Vladimir. *The Russian Plot to Seize Galicia*. Jersey City, N.J.: Ukrainian National Council, 1915.

Tanty, Mieczystaw. "Kontaku rosyjskich komitetow Slowianskich ze Slowianami a Austro-Wegier" (The Contacts of the Russian Slavic Committees with the Austro-Hungarian Slavs). *Kwartalnik Historyczny* 71, no. 1 (1964): 59–77.

Taylor, A. J. P. *The Struggle for Mastery in Europe, 1848–1918*. Oxford: Oxford University Press, 1954.

Thernstrom, Stephan, ed. *Harvard Encyclopedia of American Ethnic Groups*. Cambridge and London: The Belknap Press of Harvard University Press, 1980. S.v. "Carpatho-Rusyns," by Paul R. Magocsi.

Tonstad, Trygve. *Bjornstjerne Bjornson og Slovakene*. Oslo: Gyldendal Norsk Forlag, 1938.

Toth, Archpriest Alexis. *Letters, Articles, Papers, and Sermons*, vol. 1. Translated and edited by George Soldatow. Synaxis Archive Series: Collection 1, vol. 1. Chilliwack, British Columbia, 1978.

———. *Letters, Articles, Papers, Sermons*, vol. 2. Translated and edited by George Soldatow. Minneapolis: Archives of Americans of Russian Descent in Minnesota, 1982.

Turkevich, Benedict. *Pravoslavnoe Obshchestvo Vzaimo-pomoshchi 1895–1905*. Bridgeport, Conn., 1905.

Waren, Frank J. *The Slav Invasion and the Mine Workers: A Study in Immigration*. Philadelphia: J. B. Lippincott, 1904.

Warzeski, Walter C. *Byzantine Rite Rusins in Carpatho-Ruthenia and America*. Pittsburgh, Pa.: Byzantine Seminary Press, 1971.

Zeman, Z. A. B. *The Breakup of the Habsburg Empire: 1914–1918*. London: Oxford University Press, 1961.

Index